SENN'S
CULINARY ENCYCLOPÆDIA

A Dictionary

OF TECHNICAL TERMS, THE NAMES OF ALL FOODS, FOOD AND
COOKERY AUXILIARIES, CONDIMENTS AND BEVERAGES.

SPECIALLY ADAPTED FOR USE BY
CHEFS, HOTEL AND RESTAURANT MANAGERS,
COOKERY TEACHERS, HOUSEKEEPERS, ETC.

BEING A

REVISED, GREATLY IMPROVED, AND UP-TO-DATE VERSION OF THE
ORIGINAL WORK, ENTITLED "CULINARY DICTIONARY,"
BY THE SAME AUTHOR.

BY

CHARLES HERMAN SENN.

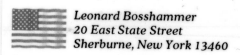

INTRODUCTION.

THE object of this little book is intended to show the reader at a glance the meaning of certain words and expressions used in cookery and gastronomy. It gives in a concise form such information which would otherwise cost much time and labour to obtain. It is a dictionary of culinary technical terms, the names of most food stuffs, food and cookery auxiliaries, condiments and beverages. The names of many new delicacies and foods will be found duly registered, whilst all the foreign terms used in menus and recipes are translated or explained. In short, every subject referring to the table or cuisine has been judiciously treated, and the so-called technicalities have been rendered intelligible.

The work is by no means complete, and I do not wish it to be regarded as such; though I trust by means of it many a difficult question will be answered, and that it will be found a helpful and convenient manual of reference by professional cooks, cookery teachers, managers of hotels, clubs, restaurants, and of households.

CH. HERMAN SENN.

PREFACE.

THE technical terms used in cookery have originated
in the language of the different countries in which
the art was practised. The words now in use are chiefly
French. In science most of the technical words are of
Greek origin. Italian words formerly more common in
cookery have been entirely superseded by French, and if
French words were Anglicised there would still be a
difficulty in finding words equally expressive. It would
be an advantage when possible in menus to use English
words as well as French, but in recipes this is scarcely
possible because no other words have the same meaning
and value ; and as cookery for two centuries has been more
carefully cultivated by the French we have a large number
of French words which are often a stumbling-block to
cooks, but when these words are explained they are no
longer a difficulty but a valuable assistance, and it is the
object of the following pages to provide persons with a
dictionary of words used in cookery. The French language
is now the language of diplomacy and cookery.

J. C. BUCKMASTER.

CULINARY ENCYCLOPÆDIA.

A.

Aal, *g.* Anguille, *f.* Eel, *e.* A genus of soft finned fish.

Abaisse, *f.* A paste thinly rolled out, used for lining tarts and soufflés, croustades, etc.

Abatis, *f.* The head, neck, liver, comb, kernels, and wings of a bird. Giblets.

Abavo. Name of an Indian pumpkin, from which a delicious soup is prepared.

Abendmahl, *g.* Souper, *f.* Supper, *e.* Last meal of the day.

Able, *f.* A fish of the salmon kind, but somewhat smaller, found on the Swedish coast.

Ablette, *f.* A very small sweet water fish, of pink colour.

Abricot, *f.* Apricot, *e.* Small fruit of the peach order.

Abricoté, *f.* Candied apricot, *e.* Masked with apricot marmalade.

Absinthe, *f.* Name of an aromatic plant, also that of a liqueur prepared from this plant, consumed as an appetite-giving beverage in France and Switzerland ; sometimes used for flavouring purposes.

    Swiss Absinthe is made from plants related to wormwood and southernwood.

Accola, *it.* Name of a marinated fish, similar to tunny-fish.

B

Acetarious, *e.* Denoting plants used in salads.

Acetary, *e.* An acid pulp found in certain fruits.

Acetic Acid. This is an acid used in confectionery, boiled sugar foods, etc. Acids are used to preserve whiteness, to give body or consistency, and to prevent deterioration of delicately coloured sugar work, etc. It is obtained in two forms—by the oxidisation of alcohol, and the distillation of organic matter in hermetically sealed vessels. Acetic acid being inflammable, great ' precaution is needed when added to boiling sugar ; it is used in small quantities.

Aceto dolce, *it.* (sour and sweet). A kind of Italian pickles, prepared with different kinds of fruit, preserved in vinegar and honey, served with meats.

Achaja. Name of a Greek wine.

Ache, *f.* Smallage, *e.* Water parsley, culinary herbs.

Aqua d'Oro, *i.* A high-class liqueur invented by the Italians in the thirteenth century. It was first introduced into France in 1533 by Catherine de Medici, who became the wife of Henry II. The predominant flavour of this liqueur is rosemary and rossolis.

Admiral. Name of a hot drink, consisting of claret sweetened with sugar, flavoured with vanilla and cinnamon, and thickened with egg-yolks.

Adragan (gomme), *f.* Gum Tragacanth, *e.* Prineipal ingredient used for gum paste.

Adschempilavi. Name of a Turkish dish—pickled meat stewed with rice.

Aeglefin, or **Aiglefin,** *f.* A kind of fish resembling the codfish ; is caught on the French coast, and cooked in the same manner as a codfish.

Aerated Bread. The name given to bread prepared by a special process, known as " Dr. Dauglish's Process." According to this process bread is made without leaven or yeast, carbonic acid gas being mixed or charged in water which is mixed with flour in an iron vessel and placed under pressure to form the dough. Aerated bread differs somewhat in taste from ordinary fermented bread ; it is preferred by many because the aroma of the pure wheaten flour is much more remarkable than in ordinary bread, and because it is free from the taste of acetic acid. The kneading and moulding of aerated bread are performed by machinery, and it is thus untouched by hand.

Aerated Waters. These are used as the basis of a large number of effervescing drinks, cups, etc. They are consumed alone or with wines or spirits. The process of manufacture is not difficult; they are made by forcing a certain quantity of carbonic acid into water, which, under pressure, dissolves a quantity of this gas, but gives off the greater part again as soon as the pressure is removed, or, in other words, as soon as the stopper is taken out of the bottle. Soda and potash waters usually contain ten to fifteen grains of bicarbonate of soda or potash, in addition to the carbonic acid. Seltzer water should contain chlorides of sodium, calcium, and magnesium, with phosphate and sulphate of sodium. Lemonade and other fruit beverages are made by the addition of a certain quantity of fruit essence or syrup to aerated water. There are also a number of natural mineral or aerated waters which are obtained from springs containing certain salts in addition to carbonic acid gases. Among these may be mentioned Apollinaris, Johannis, Salutaris, Seltzers, Rossbach, and Vichy waters.

Africaine (à l'). African style.

Africains, *f.* Name of a kind of French dessert biscuits.

Agaric, *f.* A species of mushroom, of which there are six varieties used as edibles.

Agneau, *f.* Lamb, *e.* A young sheep.

Agro-dolce Sauce. A sweet, sharp sauce, made with vinegar, sugar, pine kernels, almonds, chocolate, and small currants; served hot.

Aide de Cuisine, *f.* Undercook, *e.*

Aigre, *f.* Aigrette. Sour, piquant.

Aigrefin, *f.* Small haddock.

Aigrelet, Aigre, Aigret. Sourish, somewhat sour, sharp, sour.

Aiguillettes, *f.* Small strips of cooked meat.

Aiguille-à-Brider, *f.* Larding needle.

B 2

Ail (un gousse d'ail), *f.* Garlic; a clove of garlic, *e.*

Aile, *f.* The wing of a bird. Fluegel, *g.*

Ailerons, Airelle, *f.* Small wings of birds; fins of some fish. Sometimes used for garnishing dishes, or served as ragoût.

Airelle Rouge, *f.* Red bilberry; dark red berries used for compote, jellies, and marmalade.

Airelle, or **Myrtille,** *f.* Whortleberry. There are two sorts. One originates from America, and is very savoury, and is eaten freshly picked with savoury milk or a cream sauce. The other kind of whortleberry is a small fruit, of dark blue colour; seasoning certain dishes. Wine merchants use it to colour white wine.

Aiselle, *f.* A species of beetroot, used as vegetable or in salads.

Aitchbone of Beef, *e.* Culotte, *f.* An economical joint used as boiled meat or stews. The joint lies immediately under the rump. It is a bone of the rump, which in dressed beef presents itself in view edgewise; hence it is sometimes called "edgebone," the ancient name for aitchbone.

Ajoutées, *f.* To add or mix; also applied to small garnish or side dishes served with vegetable course.

À la, *f.* À la mode de, after the style or fashion of; à la française, French style; à la Reine, Queen style; à l'Impératrice, Empress style; à la Russe, Russian style, etc.

À la Broche, *f.* Roasted in front of the fire on spit or skewer.

Albrand, or **Albrent,** *f.* Name applied in France to young wild ducks; after the month of October they are called canard eaux, and the month following canards.

Albumine, *f.* Albumen (white of egg).

Albuféra, *f.* A lake near Valencia, in Spain. Title given to Duke of Wellington, 1812. Dishes called after his name, à l', served with a sharp brown sauce flavoured with port wine. Roast pork, game, etc.

Alderman's Walk, *e.* The name given to the centre cut (long incision) of a haunch of mutton or venison, where the most delicate slices are to be found. It also denotes the best part of the under-cut (fillet) of a sirloin of beef. The name is supposed to be derived from a City Company's dinner, at which a City Alderman showed a special liking for this cut.

Alénois, cresson d', /. Small garden cress.

Ale Berry. A hot drink, made with ½ pint ale, 1 oz. oatmeal groats, ground ginger and sugar to taste, and a little water. Boiled, strained and served with toasted bread.

Ale Posset. A hot drink, prepared with ½ pint milk, a yolk of egg, ⅓ oz. butter, ½ pint ale. The milk is poured hot over a slice of toast, the egg and butter are then added and allowed to bind. The ale is added boiling, and sugar according to taste.

Aliment, /. Food; nourishment; meat.

Alisander, e. Sometimes called Alexander. "Persie de macédoine," /. Name of a plant belonging to the parsley and celery order. As a culinary plant it is almost forgotten, but may be found in its wild state near the sea coast of Great Britain. Before celery was known this plant was used as a salad ingredient.

Allemande (à l'). German style.

À l'Allemande. As a surname to dishes is applied in many cases where the origin of the preparations are in a manner peculiar to Germany. Thus a dish garnished with sauerkraut and pork (pickled and boiled), its style is termed à l'Allemande. Again, a dish garnished with potato quenelles or smoked sausages may be defined in the same manner.

Allemande, /. A white reduced velouté sauce, made from veal stock, thickened with flour, cream, yolk of egg, and seasoned with nutmeg and lemon juice.

Allerei, y. Name of a German dish, consisting of stewed early spring vegetables. A kind of macédoine of vegetables, principally served at Leipzig.

Alliance (à la Ste.), /. Name of a garnish for entrées, consisting of braised carrots, artichoke bottoms, and small onions.

Allspice, e. Piment, épice, /. Also called Jamaica pepper or pimento. The ground ripe and dried berries of a pretty evergreen tree of the myrtle species, which grows plentifully in Jamaica. It is called allspice because its flavour and smell resemble very closely that of a combination of three chief spices—cloves, cinnamon, and nutmeg. The berries when ripe and dry are somewhat similar to black pepper, only rather larger and less pungent in taste.

Almavica, *it.* An Italian sweet dish, similar to semolina pudding.

Almond, *e.* Amande, *f.* A greatly appreciated fruit, used for a variety of culinary preparations, more especially sweet dishes and for dessert. The fruit of a tree resembling the peach-tree. It is largely cultivated in Spain, the south of France, and Italy. There are two kinds, the sweet and the bitter. Malaga and Valentia cultivate the best sweet almonds (called Jordan almonds). Those imported from Malaga are the best of the two; whilst Mogadore provides the English market with bitter almonds. The latter are used for confectionery, mixed with a certain proportion of sweet almonds. The usefulness of this fruit is equally valuable for medicinal purposes as well as in the kitchen. There is hardly another fruit which touches the fancy of one's palate so pleasantly as the almond.

Almond Icing, *e.* Pâte d'Amandes, *f.* A mixture of powdered almonds, sugar, and whites of egg or water, made into a paste. Used for cake-covering, etc.

Alose, *f.* Shad, *e.* A river-fish, highly prized in France.

Alouette, *f.* (See LARK, *e.*) A small singing bird.

Alouette farcies, *f.* Stuffed larks (boned).

Aloyau, *f.* French word for sirloin of beef.

Alsacienne, *f.* (À l') Alsatian style, *e.* A meat garnish consisting of mashed peas, slices of ham, and smoked sausages.

Alum. A salt of astringent and acid flavour. It is double sulphate of potash (called ammonia) and alumina. This is often used in the process of sugar-boiling, especially for pulled sugar used for ornamental purposes. A tiny pinch usually suffices for a pound of sugar.

Alum Whey. An invalid drink made from milk, ½ pint, 1 tablespoonful wine, a teaspoonful alum, and sugar to taste.

Amalgamer, *f.* Amalgamate, *e.* To mix several substances.

Ambigu, *f.* A meal where the meat and sweets are served at the same time.

Ameaux, *f.* A kind of pastry made of puff paste and eggs.

Amidon, *f.* Starch, *e.* A white farinaceous substance, obtained by a peculiar process from flour or potatoes. It is insoluble in cold water, but soluble in boiling water, and through cooling it becomes a mass similar to jelly, and is then called EMPOIS in French (or stiffened starch).

Amirale (à l'), *f.* Name of a garnish, principally for fish, consisting of fried oysters, sliced lobster fillets, and brown sauce. Name also adopted for meat dishes and sweet entremets.

Amourettes, Armourettes. Marrow cut in strips and crumbed.

Ananas, *f.* Pineapple, *e.* A dessert fruit of noble appearance possessing a most delicate and delicious flavour.

Anchois, *f.* Anchovy, *e.* Literally, galltincturer. A small fish, native to the Mediterranean.

Ancienne (à l'), *f.* Ancient style. Name of a garnish, consisting of kidney beans, hard-boiled eggs, and braised cabbage lettuces.

Andalouse (à l'), *f.* Andalusian style. Name of a garnish for removes or entrées, consisting of groups of spring cabbage, lettuces, and short pieces of fried sausages, served with demi-glace sauce.

Andouille, *f.* Literally a hog's pudding; a kind of French sausage.

Andouillettes, *f.* Forcemeat balls, *e.* A kind of small sausages. A salpicon of poultry or game wrapped in pig's caul and fried.

Angelica, *e.* Angélique, *f.* Is the name of a green fruit rind used in the kitchen, the tender tubular stems of which, after being preserved with sugar, are used for the purpose of decorating and flavouring sweet dishes.

Angelot, *f.* A small rich cream cheese made in Germany.

Anglaise (à l'), *f.* English style. Affixed to a dish usually implies that it consists of something plain roast or plain boiled, or that the dish is prepared in a style typical of this country, which does not necessarily follow that it must be plain.

Angels on Horseback, *e.* Huîtres en cheval, *f.* A savoury. Oysters rolled in bacon slices, grilled, and served on toasted or fried bread croûtes.

Angouste (à l'), *f.* An American garnish for meat entrées, consisting of baked eggs.

Anguille, *f.* Eel, *e.* A genus of soft-finned fishes.

Animelles, *f.* Lamb's fry, *e.*

Anis, *f.* Anise or Aniseed, *e.* Aromatic plant, used for flavouring sweet puddings, creams and pastries. In Germany it is used as one of the ingredients in a fancy bread called Anisbrod. The anise plant is a native of Egypt and China.

Aniser, *f.* To strew over with aniseed, or to mix with aniseed.

Anisette, *f.* Aniseed cordial, *e.* A liqueur.

Api, *f.* Name of a small French dessert apple.

Appereils, *f.* Culinary term for prepared mixtures; a formal preparation.

Appetissant, *f.* Appetising; something to whet the appetite; relishing.

Appetissants. A hors d'œuvre, consisting of stuffed Spanish olives, dressed on little croûtes of fried bread.

Appetit, *f.* Appetite, *e.*

Appetite. Brillat-Savarin give the following most elaborate and graphic definition concerning appetite: "Motion and life create in the living body a constant loss of substance, and the human body, which is a most complicated machinery, would soon be unfit for use if Providence did not provide it with a compensating balance, which marks the very moment when its powers are no longer in equivalence with its requirements." The great Carême, who was for a time chef to the Prince Regent in England, used to discuss matters of gastronomy daily with his royal master. One day the Prince said, "Carême, you will make me die of indigestion, for I long to eat of everything you send to table; everything is so tempting." "Sire," answered Carême, "my business is to provoke your appetite, it is not for me to regulate it."

Appetite denotes a desire to eat, and is announced in the stomach by a little weakness, combined at times with a little pain, and a slight sensation of lassitude. Meanwhile the mind is occupied with objects bearing upon its wants, whilst memory recalls such things as please the taste, or, in other words, imagination fancies it sees those things for which one longs; the stomach becomes sensitive, the mouth becomes moistened, and all the digestive powers become ready for action. This is the feeling of one that is hungry, and to have an appetite one must be hungry.

Apple, *e.* Pomme, *f.* Apfel, *g.* The original apple of this country is the crab, which is astringent and bitter. There are about three hundred kinds of apple now cultivated.

Apple Fool. A purée of apples (apple pulp), flavoured with cinnamon, clove, and sugar, mixed with new milk or cream, served as cream liquid or half frozen in glass dishes or goblets.

Apple Hedgehog. Name of a dish of stewed apples (whole), the centres of which are filled with jam, arranged in the form of a hedgehog, decorated with shreds of almonds, covered with icing sugar, and browned in the oven.

Apple Meringue. This is similar to apple snow, but is baked in a slow oven after being dressed on the dish.

Apple Pupton. A kind of apple pudding made with apple pulp, breadcrumbs, butter, eggs, and sugar, baked in a plain mould, and served with a fruit syrup (hot).

Apple Snow. Name of a sweet dish composed of apple pulp or purée, mixed with sugar, etc. This is mingled into some stiffly-whipped and sweetened white of egg. The mixture is piled high in a glass dish, and decorated with fruit jelly.

Apple Tansy. This is a kind of apple fritter. The batter is made of cream and eggs, and poured over partially-stewed apples; they are fried in butter, and served very hot.

Apricot, *e.* Abricot, *f.* Aprikose, *g.* First introduced in England about 1562. A delicious fruit, most favoured as dessert fruit; also largely used for tarts, jam, marmalade, and jelly.

Arbousse, *f.* A kind of water-melon, a native of Astracan.

Arrack. A spirituous liqueur, very common in India and Russia and other countries. Sometimes used in the preparation of punch and syrups.

Argenteuille, *f.* Name of a county in France, Dep. Seine-Oise, celebrated for asparagus. Asperge d'Argenteuille.

Ariston (a Greek word). Breakfast bit. A kind of bread dipped in wine.

Arles, *f.* A town in France (Bouche du Rhône), celebrated for its sausages. Saucissons d'Arles.

Aromates, *f.* Vegetable herbs as used for flavouring. Aromatic herbs, such as thyme, bayleaves, tarragon, chervil, etc.

Aromatiser, *f.* To flavour with spice or savoury herbs. Aromatic seasoning.

Arome, *f.* Aroma ; aromatic quality.

Arrowroot, *e.* Fégule de Marante, *f.* A tropical plant used for thickening sauces and other culinary preparations. It is said the Indians extracted a poison for their arrows from this root, hence the name.

Artichauts, *f.* Artichoke, *e.* Fonds d', artichoke bottoms. Topinambours, *f.*, Jerusalem artichokes.

Artois, *f.* Old county of France (Pas de Calais). Several dishes are called after this name. D'Artoise-feuilletage, pastry with jam ; also savouries.

Asperges, *f.* Asparagus, *e.* An esculent plant, originally a wild sea-coast plant of Great Britain. In season from April till end of July.

Aspic, *f.* Savoury jelly. À l'aspic, set in aspic, or garnished with aspic.

Aspiquer, *f.* A modern Parisian culinarism, meaning to put lemon-juice, or "reduced vinegar," into a jelly, a sauce or a gravy (Gouffé) ; the expression is therefore misleading ; the proper verb to use would be acidulating, to acidulate.

Assaisonnement, *f.* Seasoning, condiment, sauce.

Assaisonner, *f.* To season, to mix.

Assiette, *f.* A plate. Une assiette propre, a clean plate.

Assiettée, *f.* A plateful, *e.*

Assiettes, *f.* Name given to small entrées, not containing more than a plate will hold.

Astrachan, *f.* Astracan, *e.* Russian province. Name of a caviare, the best of its kind, exported from that place. (See also CAVIARE.)

Atelets, *f.* (Also **Hatelettes.**) Small silver or wooden skewers used for decorative purposes.

Athénienne (à l'), *f.* Athenian style. Larded, braised, and garnished with fried egg-plants, served with Madère sauce.

Atherine, *f.* Sand-smelt, *e.* A species of fish similar to smelts, distinguishable from the real smelt by the absence of the cucumber smell so peculiar to the latter. Sand-smelts are often passed for real smelts, and though not so fine in flavour and taste they are found to be both delicate and wholesome. They are generally dressed and served in the same manner as smelts.

Attereaux, *f.* Small rounds of minced meat (raw), wrapped in pig's caul and cooked on skewers.

Aubergine, *f.* A garden plant. Egg-plant a melongena, vegetable-marrow. Also the name of a kind of small Parisian sweetmeat.

Aubergiste, *f.* An innkeeper; hotel-keeper. À l', innkeeper's style.

Au bleu, *f.* A culinary term applied to fish boiled in salted water, seasoned with vegetables, herbs, and white wine or vinegar.

Aufour, *f.* Baked in the oven.

Augustine (à l'), *f.* Augustine's style.

Au gras, *f.* A French term for meat dressed with rich gravy or sauce.

Au gratin, *f.* A term applied to certain dishes prepared with sauce, garnish, and breadcrumbs, and baked brown in the oven; served in the dish on which baked.

Au jus, *f.* A term for dishes of meat dressed with their juice or gravy.

Au maigre, *f.* A French expression used for dishes prepared without meat. Lenten dishes.

Aumelette. Synonym of omelette.

Au naturel, *f.* Food cooked plainly and simply.

Aurore, *f.* A yellow colour, *e.* A culinary expression for dished up high. A garnish consisting of stuffed eggs, quartered, bread croûtons, and Aurore sauce.

Aurore Sauce consists of Allemande or Béchamel and tomato sauce, flavoured with chili vinegar and dice of mushrooms.

Aveline, *f.* Filbert, *e.* A fine nut of the hazel kind.

Avoine, *f.* Oats, *e.* Crême d'avoine, cream of oats. Used for soups and puddings.

Avola. Name of Sicilian town renowned for its sweet almonds.

B.

Baba (from the Polish word babka). A very light yeast cake. Substitute for tipsy-cake.

Babeurre, *f.* Butter-milk, *e.*

Babka. Name of a Polish-Russian cake. Prepared as a custard, containing fruit, almonds, etc.

Bacalao. Name of a Spanish fish speciality, consisting usually of salt cod, with a savoury dressing.

Backings. Name of a kind of fritters, best known in America, where they form a highly-esteemed dish for breakfast.

Bael, or **Bengal Quince.** A fruit of the orange tribe. Highly esteemed in India as a preserve, either as jam or as a syrup.

Bacon, *e.* Le lard, *f.* The sides of a pig salted or pickled and smoked. Bacon smoked, *e.*; *f.*, du lard fume. Larding bacon, *e.*; lard à piquer, *f.*

Bagration, *f.* A word used for high-class dishes (soups). Bagration was a Russian count, whose chief cook was the celebrated A. Carême.

Baie de Ronce, *f.* Blackberry, *e.* The fruit of the bramble.

Bain-Marie, *f.* The culinary water-bath. It is a large open vessel, half-filled with hot water, where sauces, etc., are kept so that they are nearly at the boiling-point without burning or reducing.

Baking. A mode of cooking; food cooked by a dry heat. The word "baking" is usually applied when articles are cooked in an oven or some other close structure, in which the action of the dry heat is more or less modified by the presence of steam which arises from the food whilst cooking.

Ballotine, *f.* Small balls or rolls of meat or fowl.

Banane, *f.* Banana, *e.* Fruit of the plantain tree. Used as dessert fruit; also for creams, ices, fritters, etc.' This fruit forms one of the principal sources of food in the tropics. It is eaten raw when ripe, but when unripe it is boiled and eaten as a vegetable, or baked and served with orange juice.

Bannocks. A kind of thin, round, flat cake, made with oatmeal, butter, baking powder and water. They are baked like griddle cakes, or in a hot iron frying-pan. Finally, they are toasted till quite crisp.

Banquet, *f.* A sumptuous feast; an entertainment of eating and drinking.

Banqueter, *f.* To banquet, to feast, to treat oneself with a good feast.

Bantam Fowl. A very small fowl, so called because it was originally brought from Bantam, Java. It is now largely bred in this country.

Baraquille, *f.* A large pie made of rice, chicken, and truffles.

Barbeau, Barbue, *f.* Barbel, *e.* A coarse fish, similar in shape to turbot.

Barbecue, *f.* The mode of cooking (roasting) an animal whole; a social entertainment in the open air; to dress and roast whole.

Barbe de Bouc. Plant resembling the salsify. Boiled in water or stock, or baked.

Barbel. A fish of the carp family. This fish is but seldom eaten in England; but in some parts of the Continent it is often found and appreciated.

Barberry. A small fruit resembling the black currant, both in size and colour. Largely used for preserves, jellies, and pickles; the flavour being rather acid it is not eaten raw.

Barbottes en Casserole, *f.* Stewed eel-pout, *e.*, en casserole also denotes a special process of cooking in fire-proof earthenware pan.

Barder. *f.* To cover breasts of game or poultry with thin slices of bacon fat.

Barley, *e.* Orge, *f.* Pearl barley, orge mondé, *f.* Barley bread, pain d'orge, *f.* Barley soup, crème d'orge, *f.* Barley water, eau d'orge, *f.* Barley sugar, sucre d'orge, *f.*

Barm. Yeast, *e.* Levain, *f.* The scum of malt liquor.

Baron of Beef. A very large joint of the ancient kitchen. It consists of both sides of the back, or a double sirloin, and weighs from 40 to 100 lb. It is always roasted, but is now rarely prepared, except at some festive occasions of the English Court, or at some great public entertainment. It is generally accompanied by a boar's head.

Basil. *e.* Basilic, *f.* An aromatic culinary herb, allied to thyme. It is included in the " sweet " as well as " savoury " herbs, on account of its pleasant aromatic smell and taste.

Basler Leckerlis, *g.* A kind of dessert biscuits—Bâle delicacy—richly flavoured with honey and spice, called after the town of Bâle, where they are mostly made. These delicacies are to be found at almost every railway buffet on the Continent.

Bass, *e.* Bar, *f.* A fish in season from May till September, belonging to perch family. This fish is most highly esteemed as an article of food owing to its delicate flavour.

Baste—to baste. To drip fat on roasting meat. Basting is done in order to prevent the outside of joints, etc., that are being roasted or baked from becoming dry.

Bath Chaps. The cheek and jaw-bone of the pig, salted and smoked. Thus called because those coming from Bath were first known, and the first to obtain a reputation as being the very finest. Bath still enjoys this honour.

Batons royaux, *f.* Small patties of minced chicken and game ; the favourite dish of Charles XII.

Batter, *e.* A mixture of several ingredients beaten together. Frying batter—pâte à frire, *f.*

Batterie de cuisine, *f.* A complete set of cooking utensils and apparatus.

Bavaroise, *f.* Bavarian cream, *e.* A kind of cold custard pudding.

Bavaroise à l'eau, *f.* Tea flavoured with syrup of capillaire and orange-flower water.

Bayleaf, *e.* Laurier, *f.* The leaf of a species of the laurel tree, known as the cherry laurel. Largely used as flavouring. It is generally included in the bouquet garni. Bayleaf flavour should always be used in moderation.

Bearnaise, *f.* A word much used in cookery for a rich white herb sauce. Comes from the word Béarn, birthplace of King Henry IV, who was a great gourmand.

Bécasse, *f.* Woodcock, *e.* **Bécassine,** *f.* Snipe, *e.* Dolt; a small marsh bird.

Béchamel, *f.* French white sauce. Recognised as one of the four foundation sauces. The name of this sauce is supposed to come from the Marquis de Béchamel, an excellent chef, who acted as steward in the service of King Louis XIV.

Beef, *e.* Bœuf, *f.* Boiled beef—bœuf bouilli. Roast beef—bœuf rôti. Braised beef—bœuf braisé. Beef has from time immemorial been esteemed as the most substantial food. Its mode of cooking is usually of the simplest kind, though an infinite variety of dishes are made from it.

Beefsteak Society. Was founded in London by a John Rich in 1735, and lasted till 1867.

Beetroot, *e.* Betterave, *f.* (See BETTERAVE.)

Beer—bière, *f.*—bier, *g.* A beverage made of malt and hops. First known by the ancient Egyptians, from whence it was brought to the Greeks, Romans, and Gauls. A Roman historian mentions this beverage as being in daily use under Julius Cæsar (about the beginning of the Christian era).

Beignets, *f.* Fritters, *e.* Also a kind of pancake, fried in deep fat.

Bergamotte (or Bergamot, *e.*) A species of pears, with a very agreeable flavour.

Bergamder. A species of duck.

Berle. Ache. Old English name for celery, celeriac, or celery-root.

Berlinois, *f.* A kind of light yeast cakes in the shape of balls ; similar to dough nuts.

Bernard, Emile. Name of a famous chef de cuisine who died in 1897. Was chef for many years to the Emperor William I.

Betterave, *f.* Beetroot, *e.* A saccharine root used, when boiled and pickled, for salads and garnish ; an excellent appetiser. It is of great value in France and Germany, where it is extensively cultivated, and used for the manufacture of sugar.

Beurre noir (au), *f.* Anything done in butter which is cooked to a brown colour.

Beurre noisette, *f.* Nut-brown butter, *e.* Butter melted over the fire until it begins to brown.

Biftek, *f.* The name given on the Continent to fillet steak or beefsteak.

Bigarade, *f.* Bitter or sour orange—Seville orange.

Bigarreau. The white-heart cherry.

Bigarure, *f.* Is the name given to a rich stew made from pheasants, capons, etc.

Bill of Fare, *e.* Menu, *f.* Literary, minute details, in a culinary sense ; a list of dishes intended for a meal. Menu cards were first used at table in 1541.

Bind, *e.* To make a mixture and moisten it with egg, milk, or cream, so that it will hold together and not curdle.

Bird's Nest (edible Bird's Nest). Constructed by a small Indian swallow species, found on the coast of China. There are two kinds, the black and white nests, the latter being much more rare, and consequently more thought of than the former. The Chinese look upon these edible birds' nests as a great delicacy, and often make them into soup.

Biscottes. Thin slices of brioche paste, gently baked, buttered and sugared, generally served with tea.

Biscuit. Dry cakes. Fancy biscuits are used as dessert, whilst ship, captain and others are used on long voyages, instead of bread. The name is derived from the French " bis-cuite," i.e., twice baked. Also applied to a certain dessert, delicately prepared small French cakes, etc.

Bishop. Drink made of wine, oranges, and sugar. It was very popular in Germany during the Middle Ages.

Bisque, *f.* Is the name given to certain soups usually made with shellfish.

Bisquotins, *f.* A kind of obsolete sweetmeats known since A.D. 241, when they were made by Huns.

Bitter, *g.* An essence or liqueur made from different kinds of aromatic plants, herbs, or fruits.

Blackberry, *e.* Mûre de ronce, *f.* An edible fruit, found growing wild in England. Very much esteemed by country people, and used for puddings, etc., and jam and syrup, which are considered to be very healthy.

Black Currant, *e.* Groseille noire, *f.* A small kind of grape fruit.

Blanc, *f.* A white broth or veal stock gravy.

Blanchir, *f.* To blanch, *e.* To put anything on the fire in cold water until it boils ; then it is drained and plunged into cold water.

Blanc Mange, *f.* A white sweet food. A sweet cream set in a mould. Originally a maigre soup, made of milk of almonds. It is wrong to add colouring matter to a blanc mange ; hence *chocolate blanc mange* is incorrect.

Blanquette, *f.* A stew usually made of veal or fowl, with a white sauce enriched with cream or egg-yolks.

Bleak, *e.* Brême, *f.* A small species of river fish.

Bloaters. Are slightly salted and half-dried herrings, which constitute a common breakfast dish in England. Those from Yarmouth are the best known ; they are dried in smoke, whereas the bloaters cured in Norway are salted and dried, but not smoked.

Blonde de Veau, *f.* A very rich veal broth, used for flavouring and enriching white soups and sauces.

Boar's Head, *e.* Hure de sanglier, *f.* An historical Christmas dish in England.

Bœuf, *f.* Beef, *e.* (See BEEF.)

Bohea. A species of black tea.

Boiling, *e.* Bouillir, *f.* A mode of cooking, needing little skill and much care. The process is usually effected in water or stock.

Bologna Sausage. A large smoked sausage, made of bacon, veal, and pork suet; an Italian speciality principally manufactured at Bologna.

c

Bombay Duck. A fish found in the Indian waters. It is very nutritive, and possesses a peculiar yet delicate flavour. For exportation it is salted and cured. In America and some parts of Europe it is considered a delicacy.

Bombe, *f.* An iced pudding filled with a rich custard of fruit cream, shape of a bomb.

Bon-Bon, *f.* Sugar confectionery; generally dainties for children.

Bon Goût, *f.* A much-used expression for highly-flavoured dishes and sauces.

Bonite. A fish belonging to the class of the mackerel, but larger than the latter.

Bonnet de Turquie. A kind of ancient pastry made in moulds of the form of a Turkish bonnet.

Bordelaise à la, *f.* Name of a French sauce (brown), in which Bordeaux or Burgundy forms one of the ingredients. Also a garnish.

Borage, *e.* Bourrache, *f.* An aromatic plant, excellent for flavouring lettuce salads and iced drinks, claret cups, etc. The plant has spiny leaves and blue flowers. (See also BOURRACHE.)

Borecole. A species of cabbage, sometimes called Scotch kale, as it is a well-known vegetable in Scotland.

Bouchées, *f.* Small puff paste patties (petits pâtés), so as to be a traditional mouthful only.

Bouchées à la Reine, *f.* Puff paste patties filled with chicken ragoût, invented by Marie Leczinska, wife of Louis XV.

Boucon, *f.* A kind of veal ragoût.

Boudin, *f.* A kind of small French sausage similar to black pudding.

Bouille à-Baisse, *f.* Is a kind of fish stew. A national French dish. Thackeray liked it so much that he wrote a ballad in its praise, beginning :

"This Bouille à-baisse, a noble dish is,
A sort of soup, a broth, or stew ;
A hotch-potch of all sorts of fishes,
That Greenwich never could out-do," etc.

Bouilli, *f.* Fresh boiled beef. A national French dish.

Bouillon, *f.* A plain clear soup. Unclarified beef broth.

Bouquet garni, *f.* A small bunch of savoury herbs, parsley, thyme, and bayleaves ; a faggot. It is tied up, in order to facilitate its removal after use. Used in stews, stocks, broths, braises, sauces, etc., to impart a rich flavour.

Bouquet of Herbs. Green onions, parsley, thyme, tarragon, chervil, etc., tied in a bunch.

Bourgeoise (à la), *f.* A surname given to dishes which signifies a dish prepared in a simple, homely, but nevertheless tasty and wholesome manner. It means a modest kind of home cookery.

Bourguignote, *f.* A ragoût of truffles, usually served with game.

Bourguignotte (à la), *f.* Burgundy style, *e.*

Bourguinotte (à la), *f.* This surname is applied, as a general rule, to dishes, in the preparation of which Burgundy or Bordeaux wine and small braised button onions are introduced.

Bourgoyne, *f.* (Vin de Bourgoyne). Burgundy wine. Also the name of a sauce (brown).

Bourgoyne (à la). Burgundy style, name and character given to dishes.

Bouride, *f.* A dish strongly flavoured with garlic.

Bourrache, *f.* Borage, *e.* Aromatic kitchen herb; also called cucumber herb, because it has the peculiar flavour of cucumbers.

Boutarque, *f.* Name of a special kind of caviare, very little known and not appreciated in this country.

Braise, or Braising, *e.* Meat cooked in a closely-covered stewpan (braising pan or braisière) to prevent evaporation, so that the meat thus cooked retains not only its own juices, but also those of the articles added for flavouring, such as bacon, ham, soup vegetables, seasoning, etc., which are put with it.

Braisée, or Braiser, *f.* A mode of cooking known as braising, which is a combination of roasting and stewing.

Braisière, *f.* A large stewpan with ledges to the lid, used for braising meats, etc.

Brandade, *f.* A dish of stewed haddocks.

Brandy, *e.* The name is derived from the German word "Brantwein" (literally translated "burnt wine"). French brandy, or, as it is called, Cognac, is most highly esteemed ; Cognac (Department of Charente, France) is celebrated for the excellence of its brandy.

Bread, *e.* Le Pain, *f.* First made with yeast in England in 1634. (See also PAIN.)

Breadcrumbs, *e.* Chapelure, *f.* To crumb, from "paner à la panure," to coat with breadcrumbs.

Bread Fruit. The fruit of the bread-fruit tree (arbre à pain, *f.*), which is excellent as food.

Breakfast, *e.* Déjeuner, *f.* The first meal in the day.

Break Flour (TO), *e.* To stir gradually into the flour cold liquid until it becomes a smooth paste.

Bream. (See BREME, *f.*)

Breast, *e.* Poitrine, *f.* Part of an animal next below the neck.

Brême, *f.* Bleak, *e.* A small species of river fish. Seasonable September to November.

Bretonne (à la), *f.* Brittany style, *e.*

Brider, *f.* To truss poultry and game with a needle and thread.

Brier, *f.* To beat paste with a rolling-pin.

Brignolles, *f.* A species of dark-red cooking plums.

Brine, *e.* Marinade, *f.* Used for the preservation of meat, etc., and to impart certain aromatic flavours.

Brinjaul, West Indian egg-plant, known in Bengal as Bangou, which name is supposed to come from the Portuguese " Bringella."

Brioche, *f.* A light French yeast cake, similar to Bath buns. The favourite French breakfast bun, eaten hot with coffee or tea.

Brisquet. The breast of an animal—i.e., the part next to the ribs.

Broche. French spit for roasting before an open fire.

Brochet, *f.* Pike, *e.* Seasonable October to January. A fish to be found in almost all waters ; much liked on account of its delicate flavour.

Broth, *e.* Bouillon, *f.* Beef stock or broth. An unclarified gravy soup, with or without garnish.

Brown Meat (to), *e.*, is to place it in a frying-pan with a small quantity of fat, not turning it till brown.

Browned Butter, *e.* Beurre noir (au), *f.*

Brunoise, *f.* Several soups are named à la Brunoise.

Brunois is a county in France, Seine-et-Oise Department, celebrated for the growth of fine spring vegetables.

Brussels Sprouts, *e.* Choux de Bruxelles, *f.* A kind of small cabbage seasonable from November to March.

Bubble-and-Squeak. A well-known old English dish, made of slices of cold meat, fried together with boiled and minced cabbage and potatoes.

Buffet, *f.* A place for refreshments, a sideboard.

Buisson, *f.* A cluster or a bunch of shrimps, crayfish, or lobster. Also applied to a method of twisting up pastry to a point.

Bullace. The bullace tree is a native of warm countries, but is now cultivated also in more northern regions; its fruit is a kind of plum, and very much like the damson.

Buns. A well-known kind of light and spongy tablebread. The special buns for Good Friday—"hot-cross buns"—flavoured with cinnamon and marked with a X are particularly familiar to English people.

Burgundy, *e.* Vin de Bourgoyne, *f.* A French red wine.

Burnt-Sugar Colouring, *e.* Caramel, *f.*

Burst Rice, *e.* Is to put it to boil in cold water; when boiling, the grains of rice will burst.

Bustard. A large game-bird.

Butter, *e.* Beurre, *f.* To butter moulds—à beurrer les moules. Sauté au beurre—done in butter (tossed). Butter was first used as a food by the Hebrews; the early Greeks and Romans used it as a medicine or ointment.

C.

Cabbage, *e.* Choux, *f.* A well-known vegetable; plants of several species forming a head in growing.

Cabillaud, *f.* Codfish, *e.* A sea fish, in season from September till end of April; obtainable all the year. The oil from the liver of the cod is highly beneficial for lung and chest complaints.

Cabillaud Farci, *f.* Stuffed codfish, *e.*

Café, *f.* Coffee, *e.* (the berry of a tree). A coffee-house or restaurant. A beverage prepared from the coffee berries after they have been roasted and ground.

Cafeine, *e.* A bitter substance obtained from coffee.

Café Vierge, *f.* An infusion of the whole coffee beans.

Caille, *f.* Quail, *e.* A bird of the grouse kind. Cailles farcies—stuffed quails. Cailles rôties, *f.*—roast quails. In prime condition from September to January.

Cake, *e.* Gâteau, *f.* Generally a mixture of flour, dried fruits, etc., with butter, eggs, or B.P., used to make it light, baked in tins or small patty-pans.

Calf's Brains, *e.* Cervelles de veau, *f.*

Calf's Ears, *e.* Oreilles de veau, *f.*

Calf's Feet, *e.* Pieds de veau, *f.* Good jelly can be obtained from these by boiling.

Calf's Head, *e.* Tête de veau, *f.*

Calf's Kidney, *e.* Rôgnons de veau, *f.*

Calf's Liver, *e.* Foie de veau, *f.*

Calf's Sweetbreads, *e.* Ris de veau, *f.*

Calf's Tongue, *e.* Langue de veau, *f.*

Callipash. A portion of glutinous meat to be found in the upper shell of the turtle.

Callipee. The glutinous meat found in the under part of a turtle's under shell.

Camerain. Name of a costly soup invented by an actor of the eighteenth century of that name, the price of the soup being £6. The gastronomic work, "Almanach des Gourmands," by Grimod de la Reynière, was dedicated to Camerain.

Canapé. Much used for hors-d'œuvres and savoury dishes. The word means sofa; it consists, as a rule, of slices of bread cut into various sizes, used plain, or fried in oil or butter, or else grilled.

Canard Rôti, *f.* Roast duck, *e.*

Canard Sauvage, *f.* Wild duck, *e.*

Candied Peel. Consists of the outer rind of lemon, orange, citron, or lime, encrusted with sugar, and is used as an ingredient of minced meat for mince pies and various sorts of cake.

Caneton Rôti, *f.* Roast duckling, *e.*

Caneton de Rouen, *f.* Rouen duckling. Rouen is celebrated for the superiority of its ducklings; they do not bleed them as here, but thrust a skewer through the brain, thus keeping the blood in the flesh.

Cannelons, *f.,* or **Canelons.** Small rolls of pastry stuffed with minced meat, etc.

Caper Sauce, *e.* Sauce aux câpres, *f.* (White or brown).

Capillaire. A plant. A syrup flavoured with orange-flowers, etc.—sirop de capillaire.

Capilotade, *f.* A culinary expression for a mixed hash.

Caplan. A fish of the salmon family, resembling smelt, of very delicate flavour.

Capon, *e.* Chapon, *f.* A young capon, *e.* Un chaponneau, *f.*

Câpre, *f.* Caper, *e.* Flower of an Asian shrub. They are pickled with water and salt. The capers contain much salt and a little oil. There is a sauce called aux câpres, in which capers furnish the desired piquancy.

Caramel, *f.* A substance made by boiling sugar to a dark brown, used for coating moulds, and for liquid colouring.

Carcasse, *f.* Carcass, *e.* The body of an animal; the bones of poultry or game.

Cardamomes, *f.* Cardamoms, *e.* A spice used for flavouring meat and sweet dishes.

Carde à la Moelle, *f.* Pieces of marrow braised with bacon. Served with cardes purée.

Cardes, *f.* A vegetable much esteemed in France. Mostly served as a purée.

Cardon, *f.* Cardoon, *e.* A garden plant resembling artichokes in flavour.

Carelet or **Carrelet,** *f.* Flounder, *e.* A small flat fish, in season all the year except in May, June and July.

Carême (A.). The name of a celebrated chef, born in Paris in 1784, died 1833; author of several culinary works, chef to the Prince Regent, George IV of England, and the Emperor Alexander I of Russia.

Carmine. Crimson colouring used in confectionery, etc.

Carottes, *f.* Carrots, *e.* A garden plant in its root (red or yellow-coloured). Carrots were first introduced into England by Flemish gardeners in the time of Elizabeth; and in the reign of James I they were still so uncommon that ladies wore bunches of them on their hats and on their sleeves instead of feathers.

Carp, *e.* Carpe, *f.* An excellent pond or river fish, obtainable all the year round.

Carpentras (à la), *f.* A surname to dishes flavoured with or consisting of truffles as a garnish. Carpentras, like Perigord, is a district where truffles of excellent flavour and size grow largely.

Carré, *f.* Neck, *e.* The rib part of veal, mutton, lamb, or pork.

Carte du Jour (la), *f.* The bill of fare for the day, showing the price against each dish.

Cartridge. A culinary term meaning a circular piece of greased paper, used for covering meat, etc., during the process of cooking.

Carve, *e.* Découper, or Découper à table, *f.* To cut poultry or game into joints; to cut up meat into slices, etc.

Carviol. A vegetable very much the same as cauliflower, best known and cultivated in Austria.

Cascalope, *f.* Same as escalope or scollop.

Caseine, *e.* The coagulated substance (flesh-forming) of milk and certain leguminous plants. The curd of milk from which cheese is produced. Cheese is therefore an important flesh-forming food in a concentrated form.

Casha. An Indian dish, made with maize and cream.

Casserole, *f.* A copper stewpan. When used in menus it indicates the form of rice, baked paste crust, or macaroni, filled with minced meat, game purée, etc. (See also POULET EN CASSEROLE).

Cassis, *f.* The part which is attached to the tail end of a loin of veal; also black-currant syrup or liqueur.

Cassonade, *f.* Moist sugar, *e.*, i.e., sugar which has not been refined.

Castelanc, *f.* A kind of green plum.

Catfish. A fish of the shark kind.

Catsup. (See KETCHUP.)

Caudle, *e.* A drink made of gruel, milk, and raw beaten eggs, flavoured with sugar, lemon, nutmeg, and other spices. A favourite drink for invalids.

Caul, *e.,* or **Cawl.** Crépine, *f.* A membrane in the shape of a net covering the lower portion of a pig's bowels, used for wrapping up minced meat, sausages, salpicon, etc.

Cauliflower, *e.* Chou-fleur, *f.* A delicate and highly-prized vegetable of the cabbage family. In season June to November.

Caviar, *f.* Caviare, *e.* The salted roe of sturgeon or sterlet (fish eggs).

Cavona. Name of new flavouring essence of exquisite aroma.

Cayenne Pepper, *e.* Poivre de Guinée, or piment de Guinée, *f.* An extremely pungent, aromatic condiment; it consists of the ground seeds of a species of capsicum of a red colour. It is also imported in pods known as chillies. A similar kind of condiment is known as Guinea pepper, which grows in East India, and is even more pungent than the former. Both are grown in England, and are used for pickles, etc.

Cédrat, *f.* A kind of citron-tree; its fruit is used for cakes, puddings, and ice-creams, and a special kind of oil is also prepared from this fruit.

Celeriac, *e.* A species of the celery plant. A turnip-rooted celery, of which the bulb only is used; usually served as a vegetable, stewed in broth.

Celery, *e.* Céleri, *f.* A salad plant, eaten raw or dressed as salad. Cooked, it is served in various ways, as a vegetable or in soups.

Célestin. A monk so named after Pope Célestin. À la Célestine, *f.,* from the Latin *cœlestis* (heavenly). Several dishes are called after this name.

Cendre (la), *f.* Ashes or embers, *e.* Cuit sous le cendre, cooked under the ashes.

Cèpe, *f.* Cepe, *e.* Esculent boletus, an edible mushroom, of yellowish colour, having an agreeable and nutty flavour, largely cultivated at Bordeaux.

Cercelle, or **Sarcelle,** *f.* Teal, *e.* A small waterfowl allied to the duck.

Cerf, *f.* Deer, stag, hart. Quadruped kept for venison.

Cerfeuil, *f.* Chervil, *e.* An aromatic garden herb plant the leaves of which form an excellent adjunct to salads, soups, sauces, etc. Its flavour resembles a mixture of fennel and parsley. The root of this herb is poisonous.

Cerise (la), *f.* Cherry, *e.* A small stone fruit of many varieties. Cherries were known in Asia as far back as the 17th century. Pliny states that Lucullus first brought this fruit to Italy about 70 years before the Christian era, and records that the Romans afterwards introduced the cherry tree into Great Britain. The name is derived from Kerasos (Cerasus), a town in Asia Minor.

Cerneau, *f.* The kernel of a green walnut, *e.* Usually prepared in salt-water. A red wine is also made from these kernels, called vin de cerneaux, which is to be drunk in the walnut season.

Cerneaux Confits, *f.* Preserved green walnuts.

Cervelas, *f.* A kind of a thick and short smoked sausage made of pork, and seasoned with salt, pepper, and spices.

Cervelle, *f.* Brain, *e.* A substance within the skull of an animal. Veal, lamb, pork and beef brains are used in cookery.

Chablis (Vin de Chablis). A famous French white wine, grown in and near Chablis, Burgundy.

Chair, *f.* Flesh, *e.*

Champignons, *f.* Mushrooms, *e.* A plant of the Fungi.

Chapelure, *f.* Dried breadcrumbs passed through a sieve.

Chapon. *f.* Capon; also a piece of bread boiled in soups; a crust of bread rubbed with garlic.

Charcuterie, *f.* The word means roughly slashed; but in a culinary sense it denotes " pretty tiny kickshaws " of pork, which are prepared in many different fashions. Black pudding, pig's feet truffled, smoked pig's ear with truffles, Nancy chitterlings, saveloy, pig's liver, are all items of charcuterie.

Charcutier, *f.* (from chair-cuite). A purveyor of cooked and dressed meats.

Charlotte, *f.* A corruption of the old English word Charlyt, which means a dish of custard. Charlotte Russe and Apple Charlotte consist usually of thin slices of bread or biscuits, steeped in clarified butter and sugar, and laid out in plain moulds in a symmetrical order, after which they are garnished with cream, fruit or preserve.

Chartreuse. Original meaning, various kinds of vegetables or fruit, dished up in the shape of goblets set in aspic or jelly. In its degenerate form, cooked game, small poultry, etc., are cooked and dressed in chartreuse style, either hot or cold.

Chataigne, *f.* Chestnut, *e.* Used for stuffing and sweet dishes. (See CHESTNUT.)

Chateaubriand. Name of Viscount François Auguste, a great French gourmand, born in 1769, died 1848. A favourite dish of fillet steak is called after him.

Chaudeau, *f.* A sweet sauce served with puddings, &c.

Chaudfroid, *f.* A name for dishes which are prepared hot, dressed and served cold, usually garnished with savoury jelly and truffles.

Chaussons, *f.* A kind of French round flat pies filled with jam.

Cheese, *e.* Fromage, *f.* The curd of milk coagulated and pressed. As a food it possesses very distinct nutritive properties, and forms the principal nitrogenous food of many labouring people. Its principal element is caseine, which is the chemical equivalent of the white of egg, gluten of wheat, and the fibrin of meat. New cheese, although nutritious, is not easy of digestion. Old cheese is said to promote digestion.

Cheesecake, *e.* Talmouse, *f.* A pastry; tartlets of a very light and flaky crust, with a mixture of cheese, curd, or almond, etc., in the centre.

Chef de Cuisine, *f.* Chief of the kitchen; head cook.

Cherry, *e.* Cerise, *f.* The fruit of the cherry tree. Some 300 different varieties of this fruit are now known, of which the black or Morella (*guigne*) is the best for cooking purposes. The white-heart cherry (*Bigarreau*) is the best of dessert cherries. (See also CERISE.)

Chestnut, *e.* Marron or Châtaigne, *f.* Named after the town of Castanea in Thessaly. A nutritious and easily-digestible fruit; used as stuffing for turkeys, poulards, and capons, also as an ingredient in soups, sauces, and purées. As a sweet or dessert it is also used in various ways. Chestnuts were a favourite food among the ancient Greeks.

Chevanne, *f.* Chub, *e.* A sweet-water fish. (See CHUB.)

Chevreuil, *f.* Roe-buck, roe-deer, *e.*

Chevreuse, *f.* Small goose liver tartlets.

Chicorée, *f.* Succory, endive, *e.* Used for salads, and as a vegetable.

Chiffonnade, *f.* Soup herb leaves, finely shredded.

Chine of Pork. Echine de porc, *f.* Consists of the two hind loins left undivided, and cooked whole.

Chinois, *f.* A pointed strainer with very fine holes, used for straining soups, sauces, and gravies. A Chinese fruit.

Chipolata. Small Italian sausages. Origin from an Italian ragoût. This name is also given to dishes which contain an addition of Italian sausages or a kind of mixed minced meat with which they are served.

Chitterlings. Signifies mainly the boiled intestine or gut of ox, also of calf and pig ; and small tripe. The German for tripe is *Kutten, Kaldaunen.* Chitterlings also stands for sausages.

Chocolate, *e.* Chocolat, *f.* The beans of the Theobroma cocoa tree infused by process of manufacture and made into paste, cake, or powder. The cocoa tree is a native of the West Indies and South America. The cocoa or cocao bean was held as a symbol of hospitality by the Siamese. In olden times it served as a current coin in Yucatan. Chocolate has been known as a favourite beverage as long as 400 years ago. Introduced into England in 1520 from Mexico, and sold in London coffee-houses in 1650.

Chou, *f.* Cabbage, *e.* Chou blanc, *f.* ; white cabbage, *e.* Chou vert, *f.* ; green cabbage, *e.* Chou rouge, *f.* ; red cabbage, *e.* Chou farci, *f.* ; stuffed cabbage, *e.* Chou de Bruxelles, *f.* ; Brussels sprouts, *e.*

Choux-fleur, *f.* Cauliflower, *e.* (See CAULIFLOWER.)

Choux-Raves, *f.* Kohl-Rabis, *e.* A turnip-rooted cabbage. Most excellent as a vegetable, but as yet very little known in this country. It is a favourite vegetable in the United States, Germany and Switzerland.

Chow-chow. Name of a kind of pickle consisting of a combination of various vegetables, such as cauliflower buds, button onions, gherkins, French beans, and tiny carrots. These are preserved in a kind of mustard sauce, seasoned with strongly-flavoured aromatic spices.

Chowder, *e.* A dish of American origin. It consists of boiled pickled pork cut in slices, fried onions, slices of turbot or other fish, and mashed potatoes, all placed alternately in a stewpan, seasoned with spices and herbs, claret and ketchup, and simmered.

Chrysanthemum. This is one of the latest plants added to the dietary list. Its taste is somewhat similar to that of cauliflower, only much more delicate. If shredded finely and mixed with a cream sauce it makes a most delicious salad.

Chub, *e.* Chevanne, *f.* A sweet-water fish, resembling the carp. Very little used for cooking purposes, it being exceedingly bony.

Ciboulette, *f.* Small green onions, chives.

Cider, *e.* Cidre, *f.* The juice of apples fermented and used as a drink, principally in the country.

Cinnamon, *e.* Cannelle, *f.* The inner bark of a species of laurel. This shrub grows wild at Java and Ceylon, but is cultivated in the East and West Indies.

Citric Acid. This acid is used in small quantities for boiled sugar goods ; it imparts body and prevents the sugar from getting moist. It is obtained from the lemon (citrus limonum), but is also obtained from other acid fruits, such as sour cherries, Seville oranges, raspberries, currants, etc. To be obtained in a white powder from chemists, etc.

Citron, *f.* Lemon, *e.* The fruit of the lemon tree (citronier, *f.*), or citrus limonum ; a native of the North-West Indian Provinces. This fruit has been introduced by the Arabs into Spain, whence it was spread over Europe, and is now cultivated in almost all the tropical and subtropical countries. An important culinary condiment.

Citronnat, *f.*   Candied lemon-peel.   The preserved peel of lemon.

Citronné, *f.*   Anything which has the taste or flavour of lemon.

Citrouille, *f.*   Vegetable-marrow or pumpkin.

Civet, or Civette, *f.*   A brown stew of hare, venison, or other game.

Civettes, *f.*, or Ciboulettes.   Chives, .   Flavouring herb for soups and salads.

Clams. *e.*   A bivalvular shellfish highly prized in the United States.

Claret.   English name for Bordeaux wines.

Clarification, *f.*   An operation which is so termed when any liquid is clarified.   For the clarification of stock for consommés and savoury jellies, finely minced raw meat, eggs and water are used ; whilst for sweet jellies, whites of egg and lemon juice are used for a similar purpose.

Clarifier.   To clarify.

Clear Soup, *e.*   Consommé, *f.*   Clarified double stock, being a strong broth obtained by boiling meat and vegetables.

Clouter, *f.*   To insert nail-shaped pieces of truffle, bacon, or tongue into fowl, poulards, cushions of veal, and sweetbreads.   The holes to receive them are made by means of a skewer.

Clove, *e.*   Girofle, *f.*   An aromatic spice.   The plant (a tree) is indigenous to the Molucca Islands ; generally used for flavouring meats and ragoûts.   The Dutch make a delicious marmalade from green cloves.

Coca.   Koka.   A stimulating narcotic ; a tonic and restorative ; taken along with or after food.   Coca wine has of late years come prominently into public use.

Cochineal.   A liquid colouring substance used for colouring creams, sauces, icing, etc.   It is obtained from insects known as coccus, indigenous to Mexico and Guatemala.   The insects are dried in an oven heated to 150 degrees of Fahrenheit.   It requires 70,000 insects to produce a pound of dye.

Cochon de lait, *f.*   Sucking pig, *e.*

Cock Ale. An ancient dish, made of ale, minced meat of a boiled cock, and other ingredients.

Cock-a-Leekie, *e.* A soup made of leeks and fowls; a favourite Scotch dish.

Cockle, *e.* Pétoucle, *f.* A nutritious shellfish, generally found on the seashore. The largest cockles come from the Scilly Islands, the North Devonshire coast, and the Hebrides.

Cock's Combs, *e.* Crêtes de coq, *f.* Used for garnishing rich ragoûts.

Cocoa. (See CHOCOLATE.)

Codfish, *e.* Cabillaud, *f.* A sea fish. (See CABILLAUD.)

Codling. Name of an excellent kind of cooking apple.

Coffee, *e.* Café, *f.* The berry of a shrub; a beverage made from the berries when roasted and ground.
* Originally grown in Arabia; now cultivated in all tropical countries.

Cognac. Brandy, *e.* (See BRANDY.)

Coing, *f.* Quince, *e.* A fruit used for compote and marmalade.

Colbert, *f.* A French clear soup and other dishes named after John Baptiste Colbert, a clever statesman in the reign of Louis XIV of France, 1619-1683.

Colcannon. A vegetable pie—i.e., mashed potatoes and boiled cabbage, previously fried in butter or dripping and baked. Originally a Scotch dish, corrupted from Kailcannon.

Compiègne, *f.* A light yeast cake with crystallised fruit. Also name of the French castle built by Louis XIV of France.

Compote, *f.* Stew of small birds; fruits stewed in syrup.

Concasser, *f.* Coarsely pounded.

Concombre, *f.* Cucumber, *e.* This vegetable is largely used for salads and pickles; known in Europe for about 500 years, having been imported from the East.

Condé. Name of an old French family. Prince Louis de Condé (1621-1686) was a famous field-marshal Several soups and entrées are styled "à la Condé."

Condiments. Highly-flavoured seasoning, spices, etc.

Confit, *f.* Preserved in sugar.

Confiture, *f.* Fruit jams. Also sweetmeats of sugar and fruits. Fruit pastes.

Conger Eel, or Sea Eel, is much larger than the ordinary eel and found in all the European seas.

Consommé, *f.* Clear gravy soup. The clarified liquor in which meat or poultry has been boiled, or the liquor from the stock-pot clarified.

Coq de Bruyère, *f.* Woodcock. A bird allied to the snipe.

Coquilles, *f.* Light fish or meat entrées, served in shells.

Cordon Bleu. An ancient culinary distinction to very skilful female cooks in France. It consists of a rosette made of dark blue ribbon. The history of its adoption is traced to the time of Charles II and Louis XV, of France.

Cordon Rouge. Name of culinary distinction, granted by an English society of the same title to skilful cooks of both sexes, and to others who are celebrated for the invention of valuable articles of food or drink. The badge of the Order consists of a modelled white-heart cherry, suspended by a cherry-red ribbon.

Core, *e.* To core an apple or pear is to remove the heart, which can be done when whole with a corer, and when in quarters with a knife.

Corlieu or **Courlis,** *f.* Curlew, *e.* An aquatic fowl, prepared and cooked in the same manner as pheasants.

Corned, *e.* Applied to salt boiled beef and pork. Derived from acorned (acorn-fed).

Corner le Diner, *f.* To blow the horn or sound the bell for dinner.

Cornet, *f.* Kind of thin wafers, usually made of flour, egg, cream, sugar and honey.

Cornichon, *f.* Very small cucumbers pickled with salt and vinegar ; they are served as hors d'œuvre and used for salads, sauces, as well as for decorative purposes.

Côte, *f.* A rib slice of beef or veal. The word côtelette is derived from côte, meaning a piece of meat with the portion of the rib attached.

Côtelettes, *f.* Cutlets. Small slices of meat cut from the neck of veal, mutton, lamb, or pork. Also thin slices of meat from other parts.

Cou-de-gin de Modène, *f.* Name of special kind of Italian sausage.

Cougloff, *f.* Kugelhopf, *g.* A German cake; a kind of rich dough cake.

Coulibiac. Name of a Russian dish—a kind of fish-cake mixture wrapped up in Brioche paste and baked.

Coulis, *f.* A rich savoury stock sauce; German grundsauce, i.e., bottom sauce below the fat, lean sauce of a braise or blanc.

Coullis, *f.* A smooth sauce, highly but delicately flavoured, used for soups and entrées. Also the name of a sweet cream.

Couronne, *f.* Crown, *e.* En couronne, to dish up any prepared articles in the form of a crown.

Court-Bouillon, *f.* Name given to a broth in which fish has been boiled; a highly-seasoned fish stock and stew.

Coutiser, *f.* To insert small strips or pieces of truffle, ham, bacon, &c., into fillets of fish, poultry or game, the holes to receive them being previously made with the point of a skewer. When small scallops of truffles, smoked tongue, ham, &c., are inlaid as garnish or ornament by incision, in fillets of any kind, they are said to be coutisés.

Cowheel. A great many invalid dishes are prepared from the feet of the ox or cow, as they are extremely nutritious.

Crackers are very hard biscuits; when soaked used for pies, or when crumbled for making into pudding.

Crapaudine, *f.* A grating gridiron; hence "mettre à la crapaudine," to grill, e.g. pigeons.

Crapaudine, *f.* Gridiron, *e.* Meaning browned or grilled over or in front of a fire.

Craquelins, *f.* Cracknels, *e.* A kind of milk iscuits.

Crawfish, or Crayfish. (See ECREVISSE.)

Cream, *e.* Crème, *f.* The fatty or oily part of milk. Used in butter and cheese making, as well as in the preparation of numerous sauces, soups, custards, puddings, pastry, and other food delicacies. Certain dishes are styled "à la crème," meaning that a quantity of cream has been incorporated into the mixture,

D

• before or after it is cooked. Meringues à la crème
are meringue shells filled with whipped cream. The
distinction between single and double cream is that
when milk is allowed to stand 12 hours the cream thus
obtained is single cream, and if allowed to stand twice
as long—viz., 24 hours—it is called double cream.

Crécy, Potage à la, *f.* Crécy or carrot soup, *e.* A
vegetable purée, said to have been invented by Baron
Brisse. Dishes named "à la Crécy" are generally con-
nected with carrots in the form of a purée.

Crêpes, *f.* French pancakes, *e.*

Crépine, *f.* Caul, crawl or kill. (See CAUL.)

Cress, *e.* Cresson, *f.* A salad plant. There are several
culinary plants belonging to this family. (See
NASTURTIUM and WATERCRESS.)

Crêtes, *f.* Giblets of poultry or game.

Crêtes de coq, *f.* (See COCKS' COMBS, *e.*)

Crevette, *f.* Prawn, shrimp, *e.* A sea shellfish.

Croissant, *f.* Half-moon-shaped fancy bread.

Croquantes, *f.* A transparent mixture of various kinas
of fruit and boiled sugar.

Croque-en-Bouche, *f.*, is the name given to large set
pieces for suppers or dinners, such as nougat, iced
cakes, fruits, which are covered with boiled sugar so
as to give them a brilliant appearance. The real
meaning of the word is "crackle in the mouth."

Croquettes, *f.* Savoury mince of fowl, meat, or fish,
prepared with sauce to bind, shaped to fancy; generally egged, crumbed, and fried crisp.

Croquignolles, *f.* A kind of fondant (petits four) of the
same composition as croque-en-bouche.

Croustades, *f.* Shapes of bread fried, or baked paste
crusts, used for serving game, minces, or meats upon.

Croûtes-au-pot, *f.* Beef broth, *e.* A favourite dish of
France which has been famed for several centuries.

Croûtons, *f.* Thin slices of bread cut into shapes and
fried, used for garnishing dishes.

Cru-e, *f.* Raw, *e.*

Crumpet. Name of a well-known tea-cake.

Cubet, Pierre. Name of a celebrated chef to the
Emperor Alexander II of Russia. His cooking was

such a triumph that he received so much a head to prepare the Emperor's meals, no matter how large the number.

Cuillères de Cuisine, *f.*, are wooden spoons. The use of wooden spoons is strongly recommended instead of metal spoons, especially for stirring sauces. The latter often contain certain acids which produce a black colour.

Cuisine, *f.* Kitchen. Cookery. Faire la cuisine, to cook or to dress victuals.

Cuisinier, *f.* A cook who prepares and dresses food.

Cuisse, *f.* Leg, *e.* Cuisse de volaille, leg of chicken or fowl.

Cuisson, *f.* A method of slowly cooking meat. It is finished off by cooking in its own juice whilst in an oven.

Cuissot. The haunch. Cuissot de veau, cuissot de cochon, cuissot de bœuf, etc.

Culinaire, *f.* This is applied to anything in connection with the kitchen or the art of cooking. A good cook is called "un artiste culinaire."

Curaçao, *f.* A liqueur made of the zest of an aromatic fruit resembling the orange, and cultivated in the island of Curaçao, S. America. Used for flavouring creams, jellies, ices, etc.

Cure, *e.* Saler, *f.* Saurer, *f.* Curing in culinary language means the drying or smoking of previously salted meat or fish.

Curry, from the Hindu word *khura* (palatable, eatable). Kari, *f.* An Indian condiment; a stew of meat, fish, or fowl; a sharp spiced sauce.

Custard. A composition of milk and eggs mainly, sweetened and flavoured, parboiled.

Cutlets, *e.* (See Côtelettes, *f.*)

D.

Dabchick, *e.* A small water-fowl.

Dace. A small river fish of a silvery colour.

Dainty, *e.* Friand or Délicieux, *f.* Pleasing to the palate; artistically arranged, daintily dressed articles of food.

Dampfnudeln, *g.* (literally steam-nudels). A very much thought of sweet dish in Germany.

Damson. (Sometimes called damascene, after the name of the town of Damascus.) A small black plum, considered the best for cooking.

Dariole, *f.* A kind of small entrée pâtés, composed of a compound of forcemeat or mince, baked or steamed in small moulds. Certain small tarts are also so called. The name usually applies to the shape of the moulds. Also some kinds of cheese cakes are called darioles. Kettner asserts that a dariole means something made of milk. Origin of the word unknown.

Darne, *f.* The middle cut of large fish, salmon or cod.

D'Artois, *f.* A kind of French pastry (puff-paste and jam).

Datte, *f.* Date, *e.* The fruit of the date tree (date-palm). The best dates come from Tunis. In Africa they form the basis of food. The so-called date wine, prepared in Africa, is made of dates and water, and has a certain analogy with Madère.

Daube, *f.* Meats or poultry stewed.

Daubière, *f.* An oval-shaped stewpan in which meats or birds are to be daubed or stewed.

Dauphine, *f.* A style of garnish; also name of a kind of dough-nuts, beignets, etc. Known in Germany as Berliner Pfannkuchen.

Débrider, *f.* To untruss; to remove the strings or skewers from a piece of meat or bird.

Décanter, *f.* To decant; to pour a liquor which has a sediment gently into another receptacle.

Deer, *e.* Cerf, *f.*

Dégraisser, *f.* To take off the grease from soups, etc.

Déjeuner, *f.* Breakfast, *e.* The first meal of the day.

Déjeuner à la Fourchette, *f.* A meat breakfast or luncheon.

Demi-deuil (en), *f.* A culinary expression. When white meats such as veal, sweetbreads, or fowl are larded with truffles, they are called "en demi-deuil." The meaning is "half-mourning."

Demidoff, *f.* Name of a Russian nobleman. Several dishes are introduced by this name.

Demi-glace, *f.* Name of a brown sauce ; also of a cream ice much served in Paris.

Dent-de-lion, *f.* Dandelion, *e.* A spring plant which grows in the fields ; the young leaves are used raw for salads. They are also cooked and prepared like spinach.

Dépecer, *f.* To carve ; to cut in pieces.

Dés, *f.* Discs, *e.*

Désosser, *f.* To bone ; to remove the bones from meat, poultry or game.

Dessecher, *f.* To stir a purée, pulp, or paste with a wooden spoon whilst it is on the fire, until it becomes loosened from the pan.

Dessert, *f.* The remains of a meal. Now indicating fruits and sweetmeats served after dinner. The ancient Greeks and Romans already knew this course, as being the custom of prolonging banquets.

Devilled, *e.* À la diable, *f.*

Dewberry, *e.* The creeping blackberry. A species of the French mûre des haies.

Dholl, or **Dhall.** A kind of pulse much used in India for kedgeree, or as a kind of porridge. In England it is best represented by split peas or lentils.

Diable, *f.* Stands for " devil." Is applied to dishes with sharp and hot seasoning.

Diet, *e,* Diète, *f.* Any specially prescribed food or meals for invalids or other persons.

Dill, *e.* A hardy biennial plant, possessing powerful flavouring properties, used in salads and soups.

Dinde, Dindon, *f.* Turkey, *e.*

Dîner, *f.* Dinner, *e.* " L'heure du dîner," dinner hour, in Henry VIII's time was at 11 a.m.

Dinner. The principal meal of the day, which usually comprises a judicious selection of food in season. The word " dinner " is supposed to be a corruption of " dix-heures," indicating the time at which the old Normans partook of their principal meal, which was 10 a.m. Since then the hour has got gradually later. The working classes dine about midday, the middle classes somewhat later, and the aristocracy between the hours of 6 and 9 p.m.

Dorade, or Daurade, *f.* A sea-fish, resembling the bleak (brême, *f.*). It is often called sea-bleak (brême or brame de mer,*f.*). Its flesh is white and of good taste. Mostly eaten baked or cooked in white caper or tomato sauce. It is also nice fried.

Dormant or Surtout de table, *f.* Decorative objects which are left on the table to the end of a meal.

Dorure (Dorer), *f.* Yolks of eggs beaten, used for brushing over pastry, etc.

Doucette, *f.* Name given to corn salad.

Dragées, *f.* Sugar plum, *e.* A kind of sweetmeat made of fruits, small pieces of rinds or aromatic roots, covered with a coating of icing.

Drawn Butter, *e.* Beurre fondu, *f.* Melted butter, sometimes served in place of sauce.

Dress, to. To pare, clean, trim, etc.; to dish up into good shape. Dressed vegetables indicate vegetables cooked in rich style and dished neatly.

Dubois. Name of a clever chef de cuisine of the present time, Urbain Dubois, author of "La Cuisine Classique," etc.; late chef to the German Emperor William I.

Duck, *e.* Canard, *f.* Duckling, caneton; wild duck, canard sauvage.

Dumas. Name of a famous French author, editor of the "Dictionnaire de Cuisine." Alexandre Dumas, b. 1803; d. 1870.

Dunelm. A dish of braised mutton or veal, originating from Durham.

Durcelles, *f.*, or **Duxelles,** *f.*, is the name given to a mixture of chopped mushrooms, shallots, parsley, etc.; used for flavouring sauces, purées, etc.

Duxelles, or D'Uxelles, *f.* Name of a French marquis, a great gourmand and gastronomer who lived at the end of the 17th century. Author of an excellent book on French cookery. A savoury purée (mince) and a sauce are known under this name.

E.

Eau de fleur d'oranger, *f.* Orange-flower water.

Ebarber, *f.* To remove the exterior parts of a piece of meat or fish.

Ebullition, *f.* A liquid which is on the boiling point. " Chauffer à l'ébullition " means heated until boiling.

Echalote, *f.* Shallot, *e.* Is a kind of mild onion used for seasoning soups and made dishes ; also for flavouring sauces and salads.

Echauder, *f.* To steep in boiling water. This is often done with fowls or game, as it will facilitate the removing of the feathers or hair.

Eclair, *f.* A French pastry filled with cream.

Eclanche, *f.* Shoulder of mutton.

Ecossaise (à l'), *f.* Scotch style.

Ecrevisse, *f.* Crawfish or crayfish, *e.* Lobster, *e.* An esteemed crustaceous fish. The one which lives in fresh water is called *crayfish* ; the one which inhabits the sea *crawfish*.

Eel, *e.* Anguille, *f.* (See ANGUILLE.)

Egg, *e.* Œuf, *f.* An important article of food.

Egg-nogg, *e.* An American drink.

Egg-plant, *e.* Aubergine, *f.* A vegetable.

Egyptienne (à l'), *f.* Egyptian style, *e.*

Ekneck kataif, *t.* A Turkish meal porridge.

Elderberry. A small black berry found all over Europe, Northern Africa, and Asia ; used for making wine. When drunk hot at night it is considered as a preventative and cure for colds.

Elmassia, *t.* A Turkish dish, made from calves' feet.

Émincé, *f.* Finely sliced or shred.

Émonder, *f.* When almonds are steeped in boiling water in order to peel them the French say " on les émonde."

Endive, *f.* A species of the genus succory ; used as salads and sometimes as vegetable. A native of China and Japan, but grown in Europe since the beginning of the 16th century.

Entrecôte, *f.* French name for a steak cut from the middle part of the loin or rib of beef.

Entrée, *f.* A course of dishes, or corner dish for the first course ; the conventional term for hot or cold side dishes. Also defined as dishes generally served with a sauce.

Entremets, *f.* Dainty dishes of vegetables or hot and cold sweets and after-dinner savouries served as second course.

Enveloppe, *f.* Enclosed, enveloped.

Epanada. Spanish and Portuguese term for panada.

Éperlan, *f.* Smelt, *e.* A highly-esteemed sea-fish.

Épice, *f.* Spice, *e.* Aromatic plants or their seeds.

Épicure, *f.* One addicted to the luxury of eating and drinking.

Épigrammes, *f.* Verbally, a short pointed poem. Used as a culinary term for small fillets of poultry and game, and breast of lamb or mutton, prepared as entrées. Also defined as a dish of alternate cutlets of the neck and breast.

Épinard, *f.* Spinach, *e.* Originally a Persian plant. A green, wholesome vegetable, very popular in modern times.

Escalope, *f.* Thin round steaks of veal called "collops." Obsolete cascalope, meaning thin slices of any kind of meat, usually egged, crumbed and fried.

Escargot, *f.* Edible vineyard snail.

Escarole, *f.* Name given to broad-leaved endive.

Eschalot, *e.* Echalote, *f.* Shalot or shallot. (See ECHALOTE.)

Espagnole, *f.* A rich brown sauce ; the foundation of nearly all brown sauces, classified as the main brown grand sauce, or sauce mère.

Essence. The virtue extracted from any food substance.

Estouffade, *f.,* or **Etuvée.** Expression for a way of cooking meats slowly in a covered stewpan.

Estourgeon, *f.* Sturgeon, *e.* A very large fish, usually salted and smoked.

Estragon, *f.* Tarragon (flavouring herb).

Etouffé, *f.* (Stoved.) Stewed in the oven.

Exprimer, *f.* To squeeze the juice out of fruit.

F.

Fagot. A small bunch of parsley and savoury herbs. A combination of culinary herbs.

Faire Revenir, *f.* A term often used in French cookery-books ; its meaning is to partly fry, meat or vegetables being slightly browned without actually cooking them.

Faisan, *f.* Pheasant, *e.*

Fanchonnettes, *f.* Small custard tartlets covered with meringue froth.

Farce, *f.* Forcemeat or stuffing, from the Latin word *farsum*, to fill, to stuff. From this is derived the word *farcimen*, the sausage. A farce need not necessarily contain meat, though the English translation makes the presence of meat essential.

Farine, *f.* (See FLOUR, *e.*)

Fat, *e.* Graisse, *f.* The oily part of animal bodies.

Faubonne, *f.* A vegetable purée soup seasoned with savoury herbs.

Faux (false). Used in "potage à la fausse tortue " (mock turtle soup).

Feast, *e.* Repas, *f.* A sumptuous repast.

Fécule, *f.* A fine flour used for binding soups and sauces.

Fennel, *e.* Fenouil, *f.* An aromatic plant, generally used in fish sauces, blanched and chopped.

Fermière (à la), *f.* Farmhouse style.

Feuillage, *f.* Leaves, *e.*

Feuilletage, *f.* Puff paste, *e.*

Fidelini, *it.* A kind of straight vermicelli paste.

Fieldfare, *e.*, Thrush. Grive, *f.*

Figue, *f.* Fig, *e.* They grow in the South of Europe and Asia. The Smyrna figs are considered the finest. Used fresh for compotes, and dried as dessert or in puddings.

Filbert. A fine nut of the hazel kind. A dessert nut largely cultivated in Kent.

Filet, *f.* Fillet, *e.* The under cut of a loin of beef, mutton, veal, pork and game. Also boned breasts of poultry, birds, and the boned sides of fish are called fillets.

Financière, *f.* Name of a very rich ragoût used in entrées.

Fine-herbs, *e.* Fines-herbes, *f.* A combination of finely-chopped fresh herbs, mostly used in omelets and sauces.

Fish, *e.* Poisson, *f.*

Flamande (à la), *f.* Flemish style.

Flamber, *f.* To singe poultry or game.

Flan, *f.* A French custard tart.

Flancs. Name of side dishes at large dinners.

Flavouring. Seasoning. Certain ingredients consisting principally of spices, herbs and essences, used in cookery to impart taste or flavour to food in order to render it more palatable.

Fleurons, *f.* Little half-moon shapes of puff paste used for garnishing.

Flip. A drink consisting of eggs beaten up with sugar, beer or wine, and some spirit. A favourite drink in cold weather.

Flitch, *e.* Un quartier de lard, *f.* A side of pork, salted and cured.

Flounder, *f.* Carrelet, *e.* A small flat sea-fish of delicate flavour, found in the North Sea.

Flour, *e.* Farine, *f.* Crushed or ground grain (wheat, corn, rice, maize, etc.) reduced to fine powder.

Flummery, *e.* Cold sweet dish, mainly of cereals, originally of oatmeal set in a mould and turned out. To be eaten with wine, cider, milk or a compound sauce. Dutch flummery is made with isinglass, yolks and flavourings ; Spanish flummery of cream, rice-flour, cinnamon and sugar, to be eaten with sweet preserves.

Foie de Veau, *f.* Calf's liver.

Foie Gras. Fat goose liver.

Fond, *f.* Strong gravy, meat stock, bottom, as in "fond d'artichaut."

Fondant, *f.* Melting, *e.* A kind of icing ; French dessert bon-bons.

Fondue, *f.* A preparation of melted cheese, originally made in Switzerland. A savoury.

Forcemeat, *e.*, from the French. Farce, *f.*, i.e. meat for stuffing.

Fouettée, *f.* Whipped with the whisk.

Fourchette, *f.* Fork, *e.* First manufactured in England in 1608 ; its use was ridiculed by men at the time.

Fourré, *f.* Coated with sugar, cream, etc.

Fraises, *f.* Strawberries, *e.*

Framboises, *f.* Raspberries, *e.*

Française (à la), *f.* French style.

Française (à la). This is, generally speaking, applied to a number of dishes of French origin. The term is used for dishes cooked in a simple manner as to those of the most elaborate finish. With the exception of a few grills and soups, the term cannot be taken as signifying anything in particular, because the preparation as well as the garnish varies in almost every case. **French Surnames to Dishes.**—*The French Cuisine* has a considerable number of thoroughly descriptive and well-understood · surnames given to dishes, all of which come under the title of " à la Française "; many of these are named after some peculiarities favoured in the provinces of France. Surnames derived from French towns, from certain countries, and from past and present patrons of the culinary art under whose influence many dishes have been invented and in some cases actually prepared, are also very numerous, and, with few exceptions, most significant and expressive. There are many dishes which derive their names merely from sauces with which they are served or dressed, and have no reference to the mode of preparation. Thus dishes styled à la Béchamel, à la Bordelaise, à la Tomato, à l'Espagnole, etc., are, as a rule, names merely derived from these sauces. The old school strictly adheres to these names ; they are universally adopted by all good cooks and recognised by connoisseurs and gourmets alike. It must however be stated that many of these names are either abused or misused by some cooks, many of them having their own formula of preparation, which are presented under names that differ considerably as regards the external, and sometimes internal, features from the original methods for which these names were intended as symbols of typical preparations. Dishes thus altered are therefore hard to recognise if served under a well-known name, but in a different style ; they lose all the culinary charm or its significance ; they puzzle and fog the diner who is acquainted with the gastronomic law in respect to the names and characteristics of dishes ; and, to say the least, they confuse cooks of a different type who may be called upon to prepare dishes produced and served under wrong titles, by cooks who have more chances to suit their own convenience.

Francatelli. Name of an eminent chef (1805-1876), author of the "Cook's Guide" and the "Modern Cook," pupil of A. Carême, chef at the Reform Club and to Queen Victoria.

Frangipane. A substitute for custards made of eggs, milk, some flour, with an addition of lemon-peel, rum, brandy, and vanilla, etc., to flavour.

Frapper, *f.* Iced (used when cooling champagne).

French Beans, *e.* Haricot verts, *f.* A half-hardy annual plant, brought originally from India.

Friand, *f.* An epicure ; a dainty person.

Friandines, *f.* Small round patties containing mince.

Friar's Omelet. A baked omelet prepared with apples stewed to a pulp, eggs, and sugar.

Fricandeau, *f.* Braised fillet of veal, larded. This dish is supposed to have been invented by Jean de Carême, who was the direct ancestor of the famous Carême. He was cook to Pope Leo X. This Pontiff possessed magnificent tastes ; he fostered the genius of Raphael the painter, and encouraged also the genius which could discover a fricandeau.

Fricandelles, *f.* Small thin braised steaks of veal or game.

Fricassée, *f.* Fricasseed, *e.* The word comes from the English *freak*, brisk, dainty. A white stew of chicken or veal.

Frit, *f.* Fried in butter or dripping.

Frittata. An Italian dish; a kind of rolled pancake crumbed and fried in fat.

Fritter, *e.* Beignets, *f.* Anything dipped in batter, crumbed or egged, and fried.

Friture, *f.* This word has two significations ; it applies to the fat, which may be oil, lard, or dripping in which articles are fried. Further, it is applied to anything that has been fried, such as egged and crumbed fried fish, fried potatoes, croquettes, or rissoles, being pre-eminently popular under this term.

Frog. Edible frogs are found in England and Southern Europe. The hind legs are supposed to be a great delicacy, principally in France and South Germany, where it is a favourite Lent dish.

Fromage Glace, *f.* A dish of ice-cream in a cheese-like shape.

Frosting. A culinary term; to make certain dishes appear like frost. It consists of whipped whites of egg spread roughly over the dish, dredged with castor sugar, and baked in a cool oven.

Frothing of roast joints, or roasts in general. Dredging the surface with flour, and briskly heating it to a brown colour before the fire, or with a red-hot disc of iron—a so-called salamander.

Frumenty. Once a Lord Mayor's dish, and a staple food of our robust ancestors; it is wheat or barley boiled. Eaten with honey, sugar, milk, or treacle.

Frying, *e.* Frire, *f.* To cook in fat, butter, or oil. No salt should be in the fat, nor in the food fried in it.

Fumet, *f.* The flavour or essence of game, fish, or any highly-flavoured concentrated substance used to impart a rich flavour to certain dishes.

Furcifer is the name under which the fork was introduced into England at the beginning of the 17th century. Tom Coryat first brought table-forks to England.

G.

Galantine, *f.* A dish of white meat, rolled, served cold. A fowl or breast of veal, boned and stuffed with farce, tongue, truffle, etc.

Galette, *f.* A kind of French pastry. A species of light breakfast rolls.

Galimafré, *f.* A kind of ragoût made of cold meat. Origin of word unknown.

Game. *e.* Gibier, *f.*

Garbure, *f.* A kind of maigre broth made with bread and vegetables. Originally a soup of cabbage and bacon.

Gardon, *f.* A sweet-water fish.

Gargotage, *f.* Badly dressed victuals.

Gargotier. Keeper of a common cookshop ; a bad cook.

Garlic, *e.* Ail, *f.* A root-plant with a pungent taste. Like onions, chives and shallots, it possesses medicinal virtues, being cooling to the system, increasing saliva and gastric juices, stimulating, and digestive. First imported from Sicily.

Garnishing. As a culinary term, it means to decorate a dish with edibles of ornamental appearance.

Garum. A Latin word, used for a sauce made of pickled fish, which was celebrated amongst the Romans.

Gasterea. Goddess of Gastronomy, presiding over everything appertaining to the preservation of life.

Gastronome. A caterer ; hotel or restaurant keeper.

Gastronomy, *e.* Gastronomie, *f.* The art of good living. Strictly speaking, meaning the science of life, through which we discover what food, under various circumstances, is best suited, and it teaches us the effect it bears upon man individually or a nation.—" The Autocrat of the Dinner Table."

Gâteau, *f.* A round flat cake, generally decorated. Essentially a cake made of well-beaten butter dough.

Gaufre, *f.* A light biscuit; wafer; baked or fried in specially-constructed Gaufre moulds. These consist of two opposed plates, and are worked by handles.

Gelatine. A manufactured article, used for giving solidity to liquids. (See also ISINGLASS.)

Gelée, *f.* Jelly, *e.* Inspissated juice of fruit or meat.

Gelinotte, *f.* Hazel-hen ; heath-cock.

Génevoise (à la). Geneva style.

Genièvre, *f.* Juniper-berry. A blue-black berry, possessing a peculiar aromatic flavour, used as a flavouring condiment in mirepoix, marinades, etc. ; also used in syrups and liqueurs.

Génoise, *f.* Genoese style. Also the name of a kind of sponge cake ; a brown fish sauce.

German style, *e.* À l'Allemande, *f.*

Ghee. An Indian word for clarified butter.

Gherkin, *e.* Cornichon, or Petit concombre, *f.* Term mostly used for pickled cucumbers.

Gibier, *f.* Game, *e.* Animals taken in the chase.

Giblets, *e.* Abatis, *f.* The trimmings of poultry (neck, pinions, liver, heart, etc.). Those from geese, turkeys, fowls, and ducks' are principally used for pies, stews and soups.

Gibolette, *f.* Meaning a stew of rabbit.

Gigot à Sept Heures, or **Gigot à la Cuillère,** is a leg of mutton which has been cooked for seven hours, when it may be carved with a spoon.

Gimblettes, *f.* A kind of French pastry, resembling and prepared similarly to Croque-en-bouche.

Gin, *e.* (See GENIÈVRE, *f.*).

Ginger, *e.* Gingembre, *f.* A root-plant ; native of the East and West Indies. It is ground or preserved whole for various culinary purposes.

Gingerbread, or **Pain d'épice,** has been in use ever since the fourteenth century. It was then made and sold only in Paris, according to Monteil (" Histoire des Français"). Gingerbread was introduced into England by the Court of Henry IV.

Girofle, *f.* Clove, *e.* A very pungent aromatic spice, vulgarly called " clou de girofle," because it has the form of a nail ; native of the island of Ternate.

Gitana (à la). Gipsy fashion.

Glacé, *f.* Frozen, iced.

Glace, *f.* Ice. Also applied to concentrated stock—i.e., meat glaze.

Glace de sucre (Glace royale). Icing sugar ; very fine dust sugar.

Glaced. Anything that is iced or frozen, or anything having a smooth and glossy surface, applied by means of meat glaze, sauce, jelly, or of sugar.

Glaze, *e.* Glace de viande, *f.* Stock or gravy reduced to the thickness of jelly ; used for glazing meats, etc., to improve their appearance. Well-made glaze adheres firmly to the meat. Also used for strengthening soups and sauces.

Globe Artichoke, *e.* Artichaut, *f.* A plant extensively cultivated for culinary purposes, like a thistle, with large scaly heads similar to the cone of a pine.

Glutton, *e.* Glouton or gourmand, *f.*

Gnocchi. A light savoury dough, boiled, and served with grated Parmesan cheese (Italian dish).

Godiveau, *f.*   Rich veal forcemeat.   Quenelles.   Used as a garnish almost exclusively.

Goose, *e.*   Oie, *f.*   Goose liver—foie gras ; foie d'oie, *f.*

Gooseberry, *e.*   Groseille, *f.*   The fruit of a prickly shrub indigenous to Great Britain.   The word is taken from the Scotch " Grosart."

Gooseberry Fool.   A half-frozen fruit pulp, served as sweet.   The name is a corruption of " gooseberry foul " (foulé), meaning milled or pressed gooseberries.

Goulash, or Gulash.   A Hungarian dish.   Finely-sliced beef or veal stew, highly seasoned with paprika (a kind of mild capsicum pepper).

Gourmand, *f.*   An epicure ; a ravenous eater ; a glutton.

Gourmet, *f.*   A. judge of good living ; one who values and enjoys good eating ; connoisseur in wine.

Goût, *f.*   Taste or savour, *e.*   Relish, to perceive by the tongue ; the sense of tasting ; an intellectual relish.

Goûter, *f.*   An afternoon meal ; a meat tea.   To taste, to relish.

Gramolata.   A kind of half-frozen lemon water-ice served in glasses.

Grape, *e.*   Raisin, *f.*   The fruit of the vine.   Native of Greece, Asiatic-Turkey and Persia, from whence it was spread over all countries where the climate allows it.

Gras (au), *f.*   This signifjes that the article specified is dressed with rich meat gravy.

Gratin, *f.*   (See AU GRATIN.)

Gratiner, *f.*   To brown the surface of contents of a dish.

Gravy, *e.*   Jus, *f.*   The juice obtained from meat in cooking.

Greengage.   (See REINE-CLAUDE.)

Grenade, *f.*   Pomegranate, *e.*   The fruit of the pomegranate tree (grenadier, *f.*), largely used for preserves, jellies and syrup.

Grenadine, *f.*   Small fillets of veal or fowl larded and braised.

Grimod de la Regnière.   Name of a celebrated culinary author and an able chef, editor, in 1803, of the journal called " Almanach des Gourmands."

Griotte, *f.*   A dark-red cherry, called Armenian cherry, suitable for compote and jam.

Grive, *f.* Fieldfare; thrush, *e.*

Grog. A beverage. A mixture of spirits (mostly rum), hot water and sugar.

Groseilles, *f.* Gooseberries or currants, *e.*

Gros-sel, *f.* Coarse salt, *e.*

Grouse, *e.* Coq du bois, *f.* Black grouse, or American grouse; neat cock; cock of the woods.

Gruau, *f.* Gruel; oatmeal; water-gruel.

Guava. A tropical fruit; native of the East and West Indies. The preserves of this fruit are highly esteemed in this country.

Guinée pepper, *e.* Poivre de Guinée, *f.* This is a kind of cayenne, prepared from the seeds of the ripe chili or capsicum annuum. It is also called chili pepper. Large quantities of this aromatic plant are grown in Cayenne, in South America. The name of Guinée pepper is also given to the ground seeds of dried fruit of certain plants of the same kind as capsicums, all of which have a pungent character and are the products of Western Africa.

Guisado. A Spanish dish, mostly prepared with meat and potatoes stewed together.

Gumbo. The American term for okra soup or other preparations from okra, gumbo being the name by which okra is mostly known in South America. Chicken gumbo is a purée or soup made from okra and chicken.

H.

Hache, *f.* Minced meat, finely sliced meat. (See HASH.)

Hacher-menu, *f.* To mince meat finely.

Haddock, *e.* Aigrefin, *f.*, or merluche.

Haggis. A kind of liver sausage (Scotch dish), from "Hag," to chop, or "Hachis," to mince. The modern haggis consists of the liver, lights, and heart of a sheep finely chopped, mixed with oatmeal and suet, and seasoning. This is inserted in a sheep's paunch, and boiled for several hours. Robert Burns greatly esteemed this dish, which was, it is said, a favourite dish of the Romans.

E

Hake, *e.* A kind of sea-fish allied to the cod.

Halaszle. A Hungarian fish stew.

Ham. Jambon, *f.* Name given to the hind leg of pork, when it is salted and cured, or smoked.

Hare, *e.* Lièvre, *f.* A timid quadruped.

Hareng, *f.* Herring, *e.* A small sea-fish.

Haricot, *f.* Bean. Also applied to a thick meat stew, so called from the French word for beans, from which the dish was originally made.

Haricots panachés, *f.* French beans or string beans mixed with flageolets (green kidney beans).

Harslet. Pigs. The inside organs of a pig; also their best parts, liver, sweetbread, etc., prepared and spiced, enclosed in caul, roasted and served with a sauce.

Hash. To slice or dress in small bits. Its meaning is to redress a dish, so as to mystify its origin, by the reappearance in a different form.

Hâtelet, *f.* A small silver skewer garnished with cut roots, truffles, mushrooms, aspic, cocks' combs, etc., used for ornamenting fish and remove dishes.

Hâtereau, *f.* A dish of sliced liver.

Hâteur. Formerly an officer in the Royal kitchens, whose duty it was to see that all meat was properly done and correctly dressed.

Hautboy, *e.* A species of strawberry.

Hautgoût, *f.* High flavour or strong seasoning.

Hock. The English name for German wines from the Rhine and Moselle districts.

Hodge-podge (Hochepot). Hotch-potch. A meat ragoût with chestnuts; a Scotch meat stew. A favourite dish of Scotland. It is a kind of stew made with loin chops, or best end of leg of mutton or neck of mutton, with vegetables, such as turnips, carrots, lettuces, cauliflower buds, green peas, and onions. These are boiled or stewed in stock or water with the appropriate quantity of seasoning.

Hollandaise, *f.* Dutch style; also name of a white fish sauce.

Homard, *f.* Lobster, *e.* A crustaceous fish.

Hominy, *e.* A farinaceous food prepared from maize.

Hominy. A farinaceous food made of maize (Indian corn). It is very nourishing. Derivation from the auhúminea, which is the North American Indian term for parched corn.

Honey, *e.* Miel, *f.* Sweet juice collected from various flowers by bees. French Narbonne and Swiss honey are both celebrated. The English and Welsh honey also supply an excellent table delicacy.

Hors-d'Œuvres, *f.* Small side dishes, served cold, generally before the soup, in order to create appetite. They consist of anchovies, caviare, sardines, and other dainty relishes.

Horseradish. Raifort, *f.* A species of scurvey-root of peculiarly hot flavour. It forms an excellent relish, stimulating the appetite and promoting digestion.

Huckleberry, *e.* Whortleberry, *e.* (See AIRELLE, *f.*)

Huile, *f.* Oil, *e.* The oil used for culinary purposes is obtained from the olive tree. It is used for salad dressing, sauces, for frying, etc. Provence oil and lucca oil have the highest reputation; the former is, however, considered the best. Cotton-seed oil is now much used for cheap cooking purposes, though for really good cookery it cannot be recommended.

Huître, *f.* Oyster, *e.* A bivalvular testaceous shellfish. (See OYSTER.)

Hure, *f.* Boar or pig's head; also head and shoulders of some large fish.

Hure de Sanglier, *f.* Wild boar's head.

I.

Ice. (See GLACE.)

Iceland Moss, freshly gathered, is boiled and eaten with meat as a vegetable. The jelly made of it is a nourishing food for invalids.

Ices. Supposed to have been introduced by Catherine de Medicis in the 16th century. Some assert that ice-cream was first invented by a negro named Jackson, who kept a small confectioner's shop in Soho in the early part of the present century.

E 2

Icing, *e.* Glasure, *f.*, or glace. A covering for cakes or pastry made with fine sugar and white of egg, or sugar and water, flavoured and coloured according to taste.

Indian, *e.* À l'Indienne.

Indienne (à l'). Indian style.

Ingwer. German name for ginger.

Irish, *e.* À l'Irlandaise, *f.*

Irish Moss. Carragheen. A seaweed which grows in abundance on the coast of Ireland. When cleaned and dried it is used for making jellies; it then forms an excellent dish for invalid dietary.

Irish Stew. A stew of mutton, potatoes and onions; national dish of Ireland.

Irlandaise (à l'). Irish style. This term is applied to dishes containing potatoes in some form; these are either introduced during the process of cooking or else served around a dish to form its garnish.

Ische Bone. (See AITCH-BONE.)

Isinglass. Gelatine. The former is prepared from the sound, or swimming bladder, of the sturgeon and other similar fishes. Both isinglass and gelatine are used for giving firmness to liquids, but cannot be regarded as an article of nourishment.

Italienne (à l'). Italian style. With a few exceptions the term implies that the dish is made of entirely or part of macaroni or similar paste, and in which Parmesan cheese or tomato, or both, have been introduced. Garnishing known as à la Milanaise, à la Napolitaine, à la Parma, and à la Florentine usually contain one or the other of the above-named ingredients.

Iudabah. Name of an Arab dish. Rice stewed in chicken fat, and sweetened.

J.

Jacobins. Nickname of quenelles of custard which became fashionable during the Revolution; after the restoration their name was changed to Royals.

Jagger, or **Jagging-iron.** An implement used for cutting pastry into fancy shapes. It consists of a brass wheel, which is fastened to a handle.

Jam, *e.* Confiture, *f.* A confection or conserve of fruit, made by boiling fruit with sugar to a certain consistency.

Jambon, *f.* (See HAM, *e.*)

Jambonneau, *f.* A very small ham.

Jardinière, *f.* A mixture of spring vegetables ; vegetables stewed down in their own sauce.

Jaune-Mange, *f.* A kind of egg jelly made from gelatine, white wine, lemons, sugar and eggs. It is so called on account of its yellow colour.

Jean de Carême (John of Lent). A famous cook under Pope Leo X, who received the nickname " John of Lent " in consequence of a celebrated *soupe maigre* which he used to prepare for his master the Pope. He is supposed to be the direct ancestor of the celebrated Antoine Carême.

Jelly, *e.* Gelée, *f.* Inspissated juice of fruits or meats. Concentrated essence of any kind of food, having gelatinous substance. It is obtained by boiling to a glutinous consistence.

Jerked Beef (or " Charqui "). Beef cut into thin slices and dried in the sun.

Jernik-kalwasi. A Russian dish, consisting of semolina, milk, and honey.

Jerusalem Artichoke, *e.* Tobinambour, *f.* Imported from Brazil. A tuberous root-plant resembling potatoes, but not so nourishing. The root contains 4 per cent. more water than potatoes. If put with milk it acts like rennet (it curdles the milk). Also called Girasol artichoke, a corruption of the Italian sunflower. Best adapted for the favourite soup called " Palestine " ; also served as a vegetable.

John Dory, *e.* St. Pierre, *f.* A fish found in British seas. Name derived from the French " Jaune dorée " (golden yellow), the body of the fish being thus marked.

Joint, *e.* Relevés, *f.* The grosse-pièce or pièce de résistance of a dinner. On the Continent the joint is usually served after the fish, whilst in this country it is served after the entrées.

Jolerie, *f.* A small sweet-water fish similar to perch.

Jugged, *e.* Civet de . . . , *f.* Stewed.

Jugging. Name of a form of cooking, by placing meat in a jar with just sufficient water to cover; it is then allowed to stew at even temperature in the bain-marie, or in the oven.

Julep. Ancient Arabian name for a cooling drink containing mucilage and opium, etc.

Julienne. Name of a vegetable clear soup, first made in 1785 by a cook named Jean Julien; vegetable roots finely shred.

Jumbles. Under this name pass confections of varying degrees of complication, as the name, signifying confused mixture, seems to indicate, etc.

Junket. Juncate, from the Latin word *juncus*. Name of a favourite Devonshire dish, which consists of milk turned with rennet, double cream, sugar, and ground cinnamon or other flavouring. Usually served with fruit, fresh or preserved.

Jus, *f.* Juice; broth; gravy. The juice of cooked meats seasoned, but without any liaison (thickening).

K.

Kabob. An Indian dish of stewed meat curried.

Kagne, *f.* A sort of vermicelli.

Kail, *e.* Broccoli, chou frisé, *f.* A species of cauliflower.

Kailcannon. Original Scotch name for Colcannon.

Kaimak. A Russian sweet, similar to cream custard.

Kale. An esculent plant.

Kari. The translation in French or German of the English word "curry."

Kebobs (Khubab). Name of a dish served in India and Turkey, consisting of small slices of mutton run on skewers, and grilled or braised.

Kedgeree (Kadgiori, Kitchri, or Kegeree). An Indian dish of fish and rice curried. The name is taken from Khichri, an Indian dish, consisting of boiled fish or salt fish, eggs, and rice, garnished with hard-boiled eggs, strips of chili, etc.

Kelkel. A slice of sole dried and salted.

Ketchup (Catchup, or Catsup). Name of a much-esteemed sauce. The best known ketchups are made of fresh mushrooms mixed with salt, and flavoured with spices. Tomato ketchup is prepared in a similar way, or walnut ketchup, for which unripe walnuts are used.

Kettle of Fish. Is a sort of fish stew well known in Scotland, locally known as " fish and sauce." It is generally made from haddocks.

Kickshaw, *e.* Espèce de ragoût or charcuterie, *f.* This is a name used in cookery which may be given to any dish prepared with extraordinary nicety ; but it is usually applied to such things as are regarded luxuries by the rich.

Kid, *e.* Chevreau, *f.* A young wild goat. In the time of our forefathers the flesh was esteemed as much as lamb. The meat is sweet and very tender. It is usually cooked whole, like sucking-pig (larded or barded, and sometimes marinaded).

Kidney, *e.* Rognons, *f.* Sheep's, lamb's, veal, and pork kidneys are alone considered of any account in cookery. They possess a peculiar slightly-bitter flavour, which characteristic makes them a favourite dish for breakfast or luncheon. They are best grilled or sautéed. (Somewhat indigestible.)

Kipper. A term applied to herrings, salmon, or mackerel, split open, salted (cured), smoked, and dried. (The word is taken from the Dutch *kipper,* which means to hatch or to spawn.)

Kishri, Kitchery, Kitchris, and Kitcharee. An Indian dish, generally known under the name of Kedgeree or Quitheri. It is a mixture of rice or lentils, cooked with butter and fish, dholl, etc., and flavoured with fennel, shredded or minced onions, a little spice, etc. It is a common dish all over India, mostly served at breakfast. Dholl or dhall is a kind of Indian pulse.

Kitchener. The ancient name for cook, but now only applied to a kitchen apparatus.

Klösse. German dish, composed of small light balls boiled in water, milk, or gravy. They are made of bread, potatoes, rice, and eggs, and are varied with meat, fish, or liver.

Knödel. Bavarian name for a kind of small dumpling.

Knuckle of Veal, *e.* Jarret de Veau, *f.* Part below the knee-joint ; mostly used for stews and stock.

Kohl Rabi, Knol Kohl, or **Choux Raves.** Is a turnip-shaped vegetable, which is cooked without being pared; but before going to table the outside must be carefully removed. They are generally served with butter or a white sauce.

Konomoe. Name of a Japanese vegetable.

Koofthas. Name of an Indian dish ; a mince of meat or fowl curried, shaped into balls and fried.

Koumiss, *e.* A nutritious and easily assimilated beverage, originally made from camel's milk. It is now prepared with new cow's milk and an addition of yeast, and is bottled when partially fermented.

Kromeskis (Kromeskys, Cromeskis, or Kromouskys). A Polish word, having the same meaning as croquette in French. Balls or rolls of forcemeat or of minced chicken and ham, wrapped in caul, braised or crumbed, or else dipped in batter and fried.

Krupnick. A Russian soup.

L.

Lacteal. Pertaining to milk.

Lactean. Milky, *e.*, laiteux, *f.*

Lactometer. A glass tube for ascertaining the richness of milk or cream.

Ladog, *f.* Name of kind of herring found in the lake of Ladoga, in Russia, from which it got its name ; largely consumed in Russia during Lent.

Lait, *f.* Milk, *e.* **Au lait,** prepared with milk, or in milk.

Laitance, *f.* The soft roe of a fish. Those of herrings, carp, or mackerel, are considered as a delicacy.

Laitue, *f.* Lettuce, *e.* A genus of favourite salad plants ; very wholesome and easily digested.

Lamb, *e.* Agneau, *f.* A young sheep.

Lamb's Fry, *e.*   Animelles, *f.*

Lamprole, *f.*   Lamprey, *e.*   A kind of eel.

Land o' Cakes.   A name sometimes given to Scotland because oatmeal cakes are a common national dish, particularly among the poorer classes.

Langouste, *f.*   Very large lobster ; sea crayfish (spring lobster).

Langue, *f.*   Tongue, *e.*   The tongue of most animals is regarded as a delicacy.   The meat is generally juicy and tender ; usually cured, boiled, or braised.

Lapereau, *f.*   Young rabbit.

Lapin, *f.*   Rabbit.   A small, long-eared quadruped ; its flesh is generally considered as inferior to that of the hare.

Lapins en accolade.   A brace of rabbits alongside of each other on a dish.

Lard, *f.*   Bacon, *e.*   Also the fat of swine.

Larder, *f.*   To lard, *e.*   A culinary term which means to pass with a larding-pin (lardoire, *f.*) a small slice of bacon (lardon, *f.*) through a piece of meat.

Larding Bacon, *e.*   Lard à piquer, *f.*   Bacon specially cured for larding and barding purposes.

Lardon, *f.*   A piece of fat bacon used for larding.

Lardoons are strips of bacon which, with the use of a larding needle, are inserted into the meat for the purpose of larding.

Lark, *e.*   Alouette, *f.*   A bird belonging to the finch family.   They are caught by means of nets, and are considered a great delicacy.

Lasanges, *f.*   Lasagna, *it.*   Strips of paste made of eggs and flour, and boiled.

Laurel, *f.*   (See BAYLEAF.)

Laver.   A marine alga, growing on rocks on the sea coasts.   It is cooked like spinach, and is served as an accompaniment with roast meat.

Leek, *e.*   Poireau, *f.*   Is said to be a native of Switzerland.   The leek was, and still is, the favourite ingredient for stocks, and especially in the soup known as "cock-a-leekie," of which King James I was so fond that he retained his preference for it, notwithstanding all the dainties of French cookery.   Leeks are now served as a vegetable course. National emblem of Wales.

Leg, *e.* Gigot, cuisse, *f.*

Légumes, *f.* Vegetables, *e.* Plants used as food.

Lemon, *e.* (See CITRON, *f.*)

Lemonade, *e.* Limonade, *f.* A refreshing drink is made of the juice of lemons, the essence of the peel, sugar, and water ; sometimes the white of egg and sherry is added, especially if intended as an invalid drink.

Lentil, *e.* Lentille, *f.* The seed of a plant of the same name, resembling the bean. Though of great nutritious quality they are not so much eaten in Europe as in the Orient.

Lentille, *f.* Lentil, *e.* An edible plant resembling a bean.

Lettuce, *e.* (See LAITUE, *f.*)

Levain, *f.* Yeast, *e.* Ferment, *e.* Du pain sans levain, *f.* Unleavened bread.

Levain, *f.* (See YEAST.)

Levraut, *f.* Leveret, *e.* A young hare.

Levûre, *f.* Yeast. A preparation which ferments dough.

Levûre, *f.* The froth of beer when it begins to ferment. When pressed and reduced to a dough it preserves a very long time, and is often used in confectionery and as yeast for small bread.

Liaison, *f.* The mixture of yolk of eggs, cream, etc., used for thickening or binding white soups and sauces.

Liebig Company's Extract of Beef. A perfectly prepared essence of meat. Forty pounds of lean beef are used to make every pound of this extract. Inventor, J. V. Liebig.

Lièvre, *f.* Hare, *e.*

Limande, *f.* Dab, *e.* Small sea-fish, with white and soft flesh ; mostly prepared like fried sole.

Lime Fruit is a species of small lemon ; the tree is a native of Asia. The juice of this fruit is imported into England for the manufacture of citric acid (see CITRIC ACID). Lime-juice has more agreeable flavour than lemon-juice.

Limon, *f.* The fruit of a species of lemon trees, which are more round than the ordinary lemon (citron, *f.*).

Ling, *e.* Lingue, *f.* A sort of cod fish.

Liquor, *e.* Liqueur, *f.* A liquid.

Lit, *f.* Thin slices of meat spread in layers for culinary purposes.

Livournaise (à la). Leghorn style.

Lobster, *e.* Homard, *f.*, or langouste, *f.*

Loin, *e.* Longe, *f.* The back portion nearest the leg of an animal.

Lotte, *f.* Eelpout, *e.* Very often taken for the ordinary eel; prepared like eels or lampries.

Lucullus. Name of the famous Roman epicure and field-marshal, Lucius Licinius Lucullus, 114-57 B.C.

Lunch, *e.* Déjeuner à la fourchette, *f.* A repast between breakfast and dinner. The word is derived from the Welsh *Llwne*, lunching or hurrying. Robert Burns in his " Holy Friar " says : " An cheese, an bread, frae women's laps, was dealt about in lunches."

Luting. A paste used for fastening lids on pie-dishes in which game is preserved.

Lyonnaise (à la), *f.* Lyonese style. As a garnish it generally signifies that shredded onion (fried) has been introduced as the principal ingredient.

M.

Macaroni. This is a peculiar paste prepared from flour and manufactured into tubes. It is an Italian invention. The name is said to be taken from a Greek derivation, meaning the blessed bread, in allusion to the ancient custom of eating it at feasts for the dead.

Macaroons. A kind of sweet biscuits made of almonds, sugar and the white of eggs.

Mace. A spice which grows as a sort of leafy net-work, enveloping the nutmeg—has a more delicate flavour than the nutmeg. The tree is a native of the Molucca Islands (Indian Ocean), but is also success-fully cultivated at Sumatra, Mauritius and Trinidad (West Indies).

Macédoine, *f.* A mixture of various kinds of vegetables or fruits, cut in even-shaped discs. The name is also applied to a collection of ripe fruit imbedded in jelly and set in a mould, or a fruit salad flavoured with liqueurs and syrup.

Mache, *f.*   Corn-salad, *e.*   A plant which furnishes a very good salad.

Mackerel, *e.*   Maquereau, *f.*   A fish.   Name from Latin macularelli (little spots).

Maçon.   A French wine, grown in the neighbourhood of the town Maçon.

Macoquer, *f.*, or Calebasse.   Fruit of the calabash tree (calebassier, *f.*), grown in America.   The fruit resembles the melon and has an agreeable taste.

Madère.   Madeira Wine.   A Spanish wine, very often used in cooking.

Madeleine, *f.*   A particular kind of small cakes, well known throughout France.

Magira, *Latin.*   The art of cookery.

Maigre (au), *f.*   A dish without meat.   Applied to Lenten dishes.

Maintenon.   Name of the Marchioness Françoise d'Aubigné ; born 1685, died 1719; a great patroness of cooks, a born admirer of fine cooking.   Several dishes are called " à la Maintenon."   The dish " Côtelettes de veau à la Maintenon " is said to have been invented by this lady, who was Louis XIV's favourite, and did all in her power to tempt the failing appetite of the King when he was advanced in age.

Mait, *f.*   Maize, Indian or Turkey corn.

Maitrank, *g.*   (May drink).   A delicious beverage, originally consumed in Germany—made of hock or other white wine which is flavoured with woodruff, lemon, bayleaves and sugar.

Maître d'Hôtel (à la), *f.*   Hotel steward's fashion.   Also the name of a flavouring butter, mixed with chopped parsley and seasoned with lemon-juice, pepper and salt.   Served on grilled meats.   Maître d'Hôtel sauce is a white sauce containing chopped parsley.   Dishes surnamed à la Maître d'Hôtel generally signify quickly and plainly prepared food in which parsley is used as the principal flavouring.

Mangoe.   There are many kinds of this fruit, but the

best are grown in the Bombay districts. A number of preparations are produced from this fruit, mango chutney and mango pickle being the best known in this country. Mango jelly is a very favourite table condiment in India, also a kind of a sweetmeat called amont ; the dried shreds of green mangoes are known as am-chool ; the latter is a pleasantly flavoured condiment used extensively in the preparation of Indian dishes.

Manioc. A tropical plant, from which tapioca is taken.

Manna Croup (manna kroup or manna groats). A Russian semolina, much esteemed for making puddings, very little known in England.

Maquereau, *e.* Mackerel. A spotted fish.

Marabout, *f.* A very large coffee-pot.

Maraschino, *e.* Marasquin, *f.* A delicately flavoured white liqueur, used for flavouring jellies and ices.

Marcassin, *f.* Grice, *e.* Young wild boar, generally cooked whole.

Marée, *f.* A fresh seafish—i.e., those seafishes which are sold quite fresh.

Marengo. An Italian village, which gives its name to the dish " Poulet sauté à la Marengo." The dish is said to have first been served to Napoleon I by his chef, who hurriedly prepared a fowl in this fashion after a battle.

Marie Louise. Second wife of Napoleon I, born 1791, died 1847. The lady was a great gourmand of her time.

Marigold. A flavouring herb, also known as Pot Marigold. It is a native of Spain, and was introduced into England in 1573.

Marinade, *f.* The brine in which fish or meat is soused or pickled.

Marjolain, *f.* Marjoram, *e.* An excellent kitchen herb of strong flavour, used fresh or dried for game seasoning ; also for flavouring sauces, forcemeat, etc.

Marmalade. Originally the Spanish name of jam of the flesh of the quinces, then transferred to other jams; e.g., what ought to be called orange jam is affectedly called orange marmalade, etc.

Marmite, *f.*   The stock-pot.   A copper, iron or earthenware vessel used for making stock.

Marquer, *f.*   To prepare, and arrange in a stewpan, a
piece of meat ready for cooking.

Marron, *f.*   A kind of large chestnuts.

Marsala.   A wine similar to Madeira, but made from a
mixture of different grapes ; named after a town of
Sicily.

Marzipan.   Delicate German dessert dainties made from
almond paste.

Mask.   To cover any kind of cooked meat with thick rich
gravy or savoury jelly.

Masquer, *f.*   To sauce a dish which is ready for serving ;
also to mask the inside of a mould with savoury jelly
or chaudfroid sauce when required for entrées.

Massepan, *f.*   A French dessert pastry.

Mate.   A Paraguayan tea, commonly called Maté, the
real name being Yerba de Maté ; it consists of the
powdered leaves and green shoots of plants.   This
beverage has been known to the native Indians of
South America.

Matelote, *f.*   A marine dish ; a rich fish stew with wine
and herb flavouring.   Usually prepared from fresh-
water fish—carp, tench, pike, eel, etc.

Mayonnaise, *f.*   A kind of salad of fish or poultry, with a
thick cold sauce made of yolks of eggs, oil and vinegar ;
a salad sauce or dressing.   The sauce is said to have
been invented by the chef to the Duc de Richelieu,
after the victory of Mahon (Mahonnaise).

Mazagran.   A French term for a glass of black coffee,
sugar and water.

Mazarines.   Turbans, *f.*   Forcemeat ornaments of fish,
poultry, or game.

Mead.   Liquor composed of honey and water, a sweet
drink.

Melon.   A plant and fruit of the same genus as the cucumber.   First imported into England from Jamaica.
Melons are very extensively cultivated in Egypt and
India, and in all the tropical regions.   A greatly
esteemed dessert fruit.

Melted Butter, *e.* Beurre fondu, *f.* The former name stands also for a plain white sauce, described by the French as the one English sauce.

Menu, *f.* The bill of fare. Literally the word means minute detail of courses. A list of the dishes which are to be served at a meal. Menus were first used in 1541. Pronounce "menu" as "mennoo" so that the second syllable is sounded as something between "new" and "noo."

Menu-Gibier, *f.* Small game, such as partridges, grouse, pheasants, etc.

Menu Rot, *f.* Small roast birds.

Menus Droits. Pig's ears served up as an entrée.

Meringue, *f.* Light pastry, made of white of eggs and sugar, filled with cream or ice.

Merise, Merisier, *f.* A wild cherry, wild cherry-tree. The Kirschwasser is made of this fruit.

Merlan, *f.* Whiting. A delicate fish allied to the cod.

Merluche, *f.* Stockfish, haddock, *e.* Dried or smoked.

Mess. A dish of food. A number of persons who eat together.

Mets, *f.* The meal, or dish. "Mets de farine," farinaceous; "entremets de douceur," sweet; "de legumes," vegetable, etc.

Middlings, the coarser part of flour. A common kind of flour.

Miel, *f.* (See HONEY.)

Mignonette Pepper. Coarsely-ground white peppercorns. A form of comminuted pepper, which resembles mignonette seed when sifted.

Mijoter, *f.* To cook slowly; to simmer gently over a small fire.

Milk, *e.* Du lait, *f.*

Millecantons, *f.* Name of a small fish of the whitebait kind, found in the lake of Geneva; cooked in the same manner as whitebait. In season in July and August.

Millet. A plant and its grain; indigenous to tropical countries; there are several varieties, of which India provides the best. The flower is white and is much used for cakes, puddings, etc.

Mince-meat. Meat chopped very fine. This name is also given to a mixture consisting of finely-minced suet and raisins, sugar, currants, spices, sometimes meat, and brandy. Used for a favourite kind of pastry known as mince-pies.

Mince-pie. Small patties filled with mince-meat. This is a traditional English Christmas pie.

Minnow. A very small fresh-water fish.

Mint Julep. Name of an American drink.

Minthe, or Menthe, *f.* Mint, *e.* Aromatic plant, from which a liqueur is made. It also forms the chief ingredient of mint-sauce and is used for various other culinary preparations.

Minute à la, *f.* A surname given to dishes which are hurriedly prepared ; or anything cooked in the quickest possible style. Omelets and grills come under this heading.

Mirabelles, *f.* A kind of small yellow plum, very sweet and juicy, used for compotes, fresh or dried.

Mirepoix, *f.* The foundation preparation of vegetables, herbs, and lard, for brown soups and sauces ; also for braised meats, etc. Name derived from the Duke de Mirepoix.

Mirlitons, *f.* A kind of French pastry. Tartlets with a basis of puff-paste and filled with a custard mixture.

Miroton, *f.* Thin slices of meat, the size of a five-shilling piece, braised, stewed, and dished up in a circular form.

Mitonner, *f.* To steep and allow to boil during a certain time.

Moëlle de Bœuf, *f.* Beef marrow, *e.* The fatty substance in the hollow part of bones.

Moisten. To add liquid to a mixture.

Moka. Name of the most valued kind of coffee—crème de moka.

Mont-Frigoul (Semoule Italienne), the name of a French soup.

Morel, *e.* Morille, *f.* A plant of the fungi found in woods and orchards ; said to possess great stimulating properties ; used as garniture for fricassées, and for soups and sauces.

Mortadelle, *f.* A kind of sausage largely manufactured in Bologna (Italy).

Mortifié, *f.* Term applied to meat well hung.

Mote, or Moti. Name of an Indian fish curry.

Mouiller, *f.* To add broth, water or any other suitable juice during the cooking of meats.

Mousse, *f.* A light ice-cream. Among the definitions given for the word are: mossy, froth and foam. Mousse frappée is a dish prepared with whipped cream and flavouring, frozen without working. Hot puddings are also prepared as mousses.

Mousseron, *f.* A kind of white mushroom, principally used for ragoûts.

Mouton, *f.* Mutton, *e.* Meat from the sheep.

Mullet (red), *e.* Mulet (rouget), *f.* A highly-esteemed fish called the woodcock of the sea.

Mull (to), practically means to heat and spice, particularly wine, sherry or claret, etc., etc.

Mulligatawny. An Indian curry soup ; a paste made of curry ; derives its name from two words : Tamil and Molegoo, pepper and tunnee. Derived from an East Indian word meaning pepper water.

Mumbled Hare. A dish of finely-minced cooked hare's meat, mixed with egg (scrambled).

Mumbled Hare, *e.* Minced cooked hare's meat, flavoured, spiced and acidulated, put into a stewpan with beaten eggs and butter and cooked to consistency by constant stirring.

Mûre, *f.* Mulberry, *e.* Black and white fruit of a delicate flavour, used for making jellies, syrups and vinegar.

Muscade, *f.* (See NUTMEG, *e.*, see MACE.)

Muscat, *f.* Muscadine, *e.* A white grape (muscadine grape).

Muscovado. Name given to unrefined sugar.

Mushrooms, *e.* Champignons, *f.* A plant of the edible fungi, principally used as flavouring for made dishes, and grilled when fresh.

Mussels. A kind of shellfish, very common on all the English coasts.

Mustard, *e.* Moutarde, *f.* The seeds of a plant, Sinapis

F

nigre (*black*) and Sinapis alba (*white* or *yellow*). A pungent ground seed, chiefly used as a relish or condiment. English mustard was first manufactured at Durham in 1729. The recipe was kept a secret for many years. Some traditions assert that a lady named Clements, of Durham, first introduced mustard as a condiment in 1720.

Myrtille, *f.* Bilberry. A fruit used for compotes, syrups, and sweet sauces.

N.

Napolitaine (à la), *f.* Naples or Neapolitan style.

Napper, *f.* To cover a dish with a layer of thick sauce, jelly, or jam.

Nasturtium. Indian cress. A native plant of Peru, lately acclimatised in Great Britain, the seeds of which have a pungent taste, not unlike capers. The leaves and flowers of this plant have valuable dietic properties, and make a pleasant addition to salads.

Naturel, *f.* Plain, simple. Plainly and quickly prepared.

Navarin, *f.* A stew of mutton or lamb. A kind of haricot mutton. The name is of ancient origin, being mentioned in one of the plays of Sodelle in the early part of the seventeenth century. Turnips form the principal garniture of a navarin.

Navet, *f.* Turnip, *e.* A bulbous root used, for soups, as a vegetable, and for flavouring.

Neck, *e.* Carré, *f.* The rib part of veal, mutton, lamb, or pork.

Nectarine. A fruit of the peach kind.

Nèfles, *f.* Medlars, *e.* Small, pear-shaped, delicately-flavoured fruit.

Negus. Name of a hot drink composed of port-wine, sugar, nutmeg, and lemon-juice; so called after Colonel Negus (in the reign of Queen Anne).

Neige, *f.* White of eggs beaten to snow or a froth.

Nepaul Pepper. A red pepper of the same character as cayenne and Guinée pepper, being a species of capsicum of a sweet pungent flavour. It is largely grown in Hindostan.

Nesselrode. Name of a pudding, iced, flavoured with chestnuts, invented by Mony, chef to the famous Count Nesselrode.

Niokes, or Niokies. A farinaceous dish, prepared with semolina or Indian maize, flavoured with grated cheese, cream, etc. Of Russian invention.

Nivernaise (à la), *f.* Nivernese style.

Noisette, *f.* Hazel nut; fruit of the hazel.

Noix de Muscat, *f.* Nutmeg, *e.* The fruit of the nut-meg tree; an aromatic spice.

Noix de Veau, *f.* Cushion of veal (knuckle of veal).

Noques, *f.* Small dumplings made from flour, milk, or cream, boiled in soup or salt water, and served as garnish.

Norfolk Dumplings. Often called drop dumplings or spoon dumplings, because the batter of milk, flour, eggs, etc., is dropped into boiling water from a spoon.

Normande (à la). Normandy style, with the exception of a dish known as filets de soles à la Normande, and other fish entrées. The application of this name implies that the flavour of apple has in some form or other been introduced into the composition of the dish.

Nougat, *f.* Almond rock candy. A sweetmeat made with sugar, honey, almonds, pistachios, etc.

Nouilles, *f.* Nudels. A German preparation, "Nudeln." It consists of a stiff dough made with flour and eggs, rolled out very thinly, cut up in thin strips and boiled, and served as garnish; or fried and served as sweet.

Noyau, *f.* The stone of a fruit; a liqueur flavoured with peach or nectarine kernels.

Nutmeg, *e.* Noix de Muscat, *f.* An aromatic fruit, extensively used as flavouring; its husks are known as mace.

O.

Oatmeal, *e.* Avoine, *f.* The grain of the oat dried in a kiln and ground. There are three kinds—coarse, medium, and fine. Oatmeal when cooked is considered the most perfect example of a complete food. Generally eaten in the form of porridge or gruel.

Œuf, *f.* Egg, *e.* An important article of diet, and the most convenient culinary dish.

Oie, *f.* Goose, *e.* An aquatic domestic bird ; a favourite dish in the autumn and winter.

Oignon, *f.* Onion, *e.* A vegetable plant of the allium family ; a valuable culinary adjunct for flavouring and garnishing purposes.

Oil, *e.* (See HUILE, *f.*)

Olive, *f.* Olive, *e.* Fruit of the oil tree, used as hors-d'œuvres, and as garnish for sauces, stews, salads, etc.

Okra. Name of a vegetable extensively used in South America.

Olla. Name of a Spanish meat and vegetable ragoût.

Omble. Name of an excellent sweet-water fish, from the Lake of Geneva, weighing up to 15 lb. apiece; in season during the months of January and February.

Ombre Chevalier, *f.* Grayling, *e.* A sweet-water fish, similar to the trout.

Omelette, *f.* Omelet, *e.* A pancake or fritter of eggs, etc. Its name is supposed to be derived from the word "ovum," an egg, meaning "œufs mêlés." A mixture of eggs.

Onion, *e.* A plant of the onion tribe, the leek, shallot, and garlic being of the same species. After salt, the onion is the most valuable seasoning in cookery; it possesses stimulating and digestive properties.

Orange. This well-known fruit is principally imported from Sicily, Spain, Portugal, and Malta. The Seville orange is used for making marmalade.

Orangeade. A drink made of orange-juice.

Orangeat, *f.* Candied orange peel, *e.*

Orgeate, *f.* Barley water or almond milk ; a favourite summer drink.

Orloff. A number of dishes or the garniture thereof are thus styled. Orloff is the name of a magnificent diamond, owned by the Russian Count Alexis Orloff, who was known to be a great gourmand and epicure of the first water.

Orly, also **Horly.** Name given to dishes prepared in a certain style. Usually slices of fish or meat dipped in a rich batter and fried in fat.

Ortolan. *f.* Ortolan, *e.* A bird of the size of a lark.

Oseille, *f.* Sorrel, *e.* A sour plant of green colour, used for soups or as a vegetable.

Ox-tail, *e.* Queue de bœuf, *f.* Ox-tail soup is said to have been discovered as follows. During the Reign of Terror in Paris, in 1793, many of the nobility were reduced to starvation and beggary. The abbatoirs sent their hides fresh to the tanneries without removing the tails, and in cleaning them the tails were thrown away. One of these noble beggars asked for a tail, which was willingly given him; he took it to his lodgings and made—what is now famous—the first dish of ox-tail soup. He told others of his good luck, and they annoyed the tanners so much that a price was put on ox-tails.

Oyster, *e.* Huître, *f.* A bivalvular testaceous shellfish, highly esteemed on account of its delicious flavour and nutritive qualities. In season from September to April.

Oyster Plant. Salsify (Salsifits), a well-known vegetable plant belonging to the same class as the chicory; the flavour of the root is said to resemble that of asparagus.

P.

Pabrica. The fleshy fruit of the green and red mild capsicum, grown in the South of Europe, and used as spice for ragoûts or salads.

Paillasse, *f.* A grill over hot cinders.

Pain, *f.* Bread; forcemeat; fruit purée, etc.

Pain d'Épice, *f.* A kind of gingerbread.

Palais de Bœuf, *f.* Ox-palate, *e.*

Panaché, *f.* Mixed with two or more kinds of vegetables, fruits, etc.; also creams.

Panada. A culinary paste of flour and water or soaked bread, used in the preparation of forcemeat and stuffing.

Panais, *f.* Parsnip, *e.* A plant of the carrot family.

Pancake, *e.* Panequets or crêpes, *f.* Thin flat cakes, made of batter and fried in a pan; well-known in connection with Shrove-Tuesday.

Pancalier. A kind of spring cabbage; its name is derived from the town of Pancagliere in Italy, from whence it was brought to the royal gardens at Versailles by La Quintine, first gardener to Louis XIV.

Paner, *f.* To egg and breadcrumb.

Pannequets, or **Crêpes,** *f.* Pancakes.

Panurette. A preparation of grated rusks, used for crumbing, for coating the inside of moulds, and for decoration in place of lobster coral.

Paon, *f.* Peacock, *e.* A fowl of the pheasant kind. In olden times this bird formed a dish of equal importance as the boar's head in English Christmas fare.

Papaw. Name of an edible fruit well known in South America; very similar in appearance to a small melon, and somewhat of that flavour. It is a kind of vegetable pepsin, and is said to possess wonderful digestive properties.

Papillotes (en), *f.* Paper capsules, greased, and fastened round cutlets, etc. Buttered paper answers the same purpose when twisted along the edges.

Paprika. Hungarian red pepper. A kind of sweet capsicum of a brilliant scarlet colour; it is less pungent than the Spanish pepper.

Parboil. To half or partly cook in boiling water.

Parisienne (à la), *f.* Parisian style. A surname applied to various kinds of dishes, principally meat dishes, which are dressed in a more or less elaborate style. No particular specification as to garnish or mode of cooking can be given, as these vary in almost every dish thus styled.

Parmentier (Antoine Augustin). Born 1737, died 1813; introducer of the potato into France, in 1786, during the reign of Louis XVI. He also invented twenty different ways of cooking potatoes. Sir W. Raleigh brought the potato from America to England in 1586.

Parmesan. Name of an Italian cheese, largely used for culinary purposes.

Parr. The name given to a very young salmon.

Parsley. Persil, *f.* Is a native plant of Sardinia, and was first introduced into England in 1548. Parsley is used for sauces, salads, and as a pot-herb, and makes the prettiest garnish for dishes.

Parson's Nose. This name is given to the extreme end portion of the tail of a fowl.

Pass, *e.* Passer, *f.* A word much used in cookery. To pass a sauce, soup, vegetable or meat, means to run it through a tammy cloth, sieve, or strainer. In the culinary language the word " passer " has also the same meaning as " faire revenir," i.e., to slightly fry in butter over a quick fire so as to form a crusty surface on meats or vegetables which are intended to be finished by some other process of cooking (usually stewing or braising).

Pastèque, *f.* A water-melon, a very refreshing fruit.

Pastry, *e.* Patisserie, *f.* Usually a mixture of flour, salt, fat, and water, used to cover pies, etc. Also means all kinds of fancy tartlets.

Pâté, *f.* A pie; pasty; a savoury meat pasty, or a raised pie.

Pâte, *f.* Paste ; dough.

Pâte croquante, *f.* Crisp almond and sugar paste.

Pâté de Foie Gras, *f.* A well-known delicacy prepared from the livers of fat geese. Alsace is the most celebrated country where the so-called terrines de foie gras are made. This delicacy was first introduced by a cook named Close.

Pâté de Périgord. Name of a French pie, which derives its name from Périgueux, a place celebrated for its truffles.

Pâte feuilletée, *f.* Puff paste.

Pâte friseé, *f.* Short paste.

Pâte pastillage, *f.* Gum paste.

Pâtisser, *f.* To make pastry, *e.*

Pâtisserie, *f.* Pastry, *e.* A pastrycook's business.

Pâtissier, *f.* Pastrycook, *e.*

Paupiettes, *f.* Slices of meat rolled with forcemeat.

Pavot, *f.* Poppy, *e.* The seeds of this plant are used in stuffing mixtures and cakes.

Paysanne (à la), *f.* Peasant's fashion. Prepared in a homely way.

Peacock, *e.* (See Paon, *f.*)

Pêche, *f.* Peach, *e.* A delicious juicy fruit, used for desserts and compote. This fruit was originally introduced to Europe from Persia by the Romans.

Penguin. A genus of sea-fowls.

Pepper, *e.* Poivre, *f.* The berry of an Oriental shrub. A pungent aromatic condiment consumed with all kinds of meat and vegetables. Mignonette pepper is obtained from the seeds within the berries; it is not nearly so pungent as the black pepper. The difference between the black and white pepper is that in the latter the outer husk of the seed is removed, whilst the former is ground whole.

Pepper Pot. A West Indian dish, consisting of stewed pickled pork or bacon, shellfish, rice, vegetables, and aromatic herbs, highly seasoned with cayenne and other peppers.

Perch, *e.* Perche, *f.* An excellent small river fish. Seasonable July to October.

Perdrix, *f.* A full-grown partridge (ptarmigan). Seasonable September to February.

Perigord, or **Périgneux (à la),** *f.* Perigord style. This name is applied to dishes wherein a truffle sauce or a garniture consisting of truffles has been used.

Perry. Name of a beverage made of pears, corresponding to the cider made of apples. It contains but little alcohol, and when preserved in casks or bottles it keeps good for some years.

Persil, *f.* Parsley, *e.* A plant used for flavouring and garnishing. (See Parsley.)

Persillade, *f.* A thick white sauce, in which a large quantity of parsley is used.

Petit Lait, *f.* Whey, *e.* The thin part of milk.

Petits Pains, Purée, *f.* Very small rolls scooped out and stuffed with various kinds of savoury purées; served as savoury or side dishes.

Petits Pois Verts, *f.* Small green peas.

Pheasant. Faisan, *f.* A bird much esteemed for its delicate flavour. In season October to February.

Pichaithly Bannock. Name of a kind of Scotch short bread, consisting of flat round cakes, the paste being made up with flour, butter, sugar, almonds, peel, and carraway seed.

Pickle (to). To preserve fruit, vegetables, fish, or meat, in vinegar, brine, or in dissolved salt.

Picnic. An outing into the country, or a party outdoors to which each member contributes some article of diet. An *al fresco* meal.

Pie. A quantity of meat or fruit baked in a dish covered with pastry.

Pièce de Résistance. The principal joint or other important dish of a dinner.

Pike, *e.* Brochet, *f.* A fish known for its voracity, found in all the European lakes and rivers. Seasonable October to January.

Pilau. Turkish national dish, made of rice and onions, etc.

Pilaw. An Indian dish made of fish or meat and rice.

Pilchard. A fish which resembles the herring, but is much smaller.

Pimento. Allspice. A condiment possessing the combined flavours of cinnamon, nutmeg and cloves.

Pineapple, *e.* Ananas, *f.* A much esteemed dessert fruit, native of South America, from whence it was first imported to Europe about the middle of the XVIIth century. Pineapples are now largely cultivated in England.

Pinole. A kind of wheat-corn roasted. Used as a substitute for coffee in the East.

Pintade, *f.* Guinea-fowl, *e.* A bird of the turkey species of bluish-grey plumage, sprinkled with round white spots.

Pintail, *e.* Pilet, *f.* Sea pheasant, a common migratory bird found in the North of England, Germany and Holland.

Piping. A kind of decoration made of royal icing, used for ornamenting cakes, pastry, etc.

Piquante, *f.* Sharp of flavour, stimulating, pungent or sour.

Piquer (Piquée), *f.* Larded, *e.* To insert narrow strips of fat bacon, truffles, tongue, etc., into lean meat, poultry, game or fish.

Pistaches, *f.* Pistachios, *e.* Kernels of the nut of the turpentine tree, used for flavouring and garnishing galantines, sweets, etc.

Plaice, *e.* Plie, *f.* A flat sea-fish, seasonable May to November.

Pluche, *f.* A garniture for soups. The leaves of parsley, chervil, tarragon, lettuce, sorrel, cut into fine shreds.

Pluvier, *f.* Plover, *e.* A bird whose eggs are esteemed a great delicacy. In season October to February.

Poach (to), *e.* Pocher, *f.* To parboil or to boil slightly. Mode of cooking usually applied to eggs and quenelles of fish, meat or game.

Poêle, *f.* A cooking pot or pan.

Poêler, *f.* A mode of braising meat, etc., in a fireproof earthenware pan.

Poireau, *f.* Leek, *e.* Soup vegetable, belonging to the allium family, supposed to be of Swiss origin.

Poires, *f.* Pears, *e.* A well-known fruit of many varieties, used as dessert and for stewing.

Poisson, *f.* Fish, *e.* An animal living in water. There are two varieties, i.e., sweet-water and salt-water fish.

Poivre, *f.* Pepper, *e.* A pungent aromatic seasoning condiment.

Polenta. A standard Italian dish made of Indian corn flour. In appearance and taste it is not unlike semolina.

Pollock, *e.* Morue, *f.* A sea fish of the cod family.

Pollo con Formaggio. Name of an Italian dish, composed of stewed chicken, highly flavoured with Parmesan cheese.

Pollocowarroz. Name of an Italian dish consisting chiefly of rice stewed in broth (stock).

Polonaise (à la), *f.* Polish style. There are two kinds of dishes known under this name. The first is a kind of gratin style (baked), differing somewhat from the ordinary way of baking " au gratin." The other is the more generally known, but little appreciated in this country, its characteristic being to introduce the red juices of pickled beetroot and red cabbage and sour cream into various dishes. Borsch à la Polonaise and ragoûts à la Polonaise are types of dishes to which this peculiar flavour is applicable.

Polony. A dry sausage made of meat partly cooked.

Pomegranate, *e.* (See GRENADE, *f.*)

Pommes, *f.* (See APPLES.)

Pommes d'Api. Small rosy apples named after the Roman Appius.

Pommes de Terre, *f.* (See POTATOES, *e.*)

Pompadour (Jeanne Antoinette, Marquise de); born 1721, died 1764 ; well known for her extravagance and indulgence in the luxury of pleasure and eating.

Poncire, *f.* A large, thick-rinded lemon.

Porc, *f.* Pork, *e.* Du porc frais, *f.* Fresh pork, *e.*

Porridge. A Scotch dish. Oatmeal porridge is an every-day article of diet of the Scottish peasantry. It is both an agreeable as well as a nutritious article of food, served with milk, butter, salt and cream ; also with sugar or treacle.

Porringer. Name of a small dish used for cooking porridge.

Porterhouse Steak. A thick steak cut from the middle of the ribs of beef.

Posset. Hot milk curdled with wine or acid ; from the Welsh *posel,* curdled milk.

Potage, *f.* Soup, *e.* A nourishing broth or liquor, forming the first course of a dinner.

Potato. Potatoes were first introduced into Europe in 1584 by Thomas Heriot, and were for a long time after considered as a great delicacy, and could only be procured in small quantities at the price of 2s. per pound. After the middle of the seventeenth century they became gradually known and more extensively cultivated. As diet it closely resembles rice.

Pot-au-feu, *f.,* is an economical and wholesome beef broth. It is the standard dish of all classes in France, and the origin of beef stock.

Potiron, *f.* Pumpkin or pompion. The fruit of an annual plant belonging to the gourd family.

Potpourri. A stew of various kinds of meats and spices ; a favourite dish in Spain.

Potrock. Name of a Russian thick soup.

Potted. Fish or meat purée preserved in a pot.

Pottinger. Ancient popular name of apothecary or spice merchant.

Poularde, *f.* A very fat fowl or fine pullet.

Poule, *f.* A hen, *e.* A fowl.

Poule-au-pot, *f.* Boiled fowl cooked in the stock-pot.

Poule de Neige, *f.* White grouse, *e.*

Poulet, *f.* A young chicken, *e.*

Poulet de Grain, *f.* A young cock (boy chicken).

Poulet en casserole. Chicken fried and basted with butter in an earthenware stewpan. When the chicken is browned in the butter the lid is put on the stewpan and it is allowed to cook slowly until done, being basted occasionally.

Poulets à la Reine, *f.* Name given to fine specimens of young chickens.

Poulette, *f.* A young hen, *e.* A sauce made of flour, stock, butter, and chopped herbs, used for the dishes prepared " à la poulette."

Poulpeton, or **Polpetti.** Slices of veal with minced meat.

Poupelin, *f.* A kind of pastry.

Poupeton, *f.* A kind of pie made of hashed meat or fish.

Pourpier, *f.* (See PURSLANE, *e.*)

Poussin, *f.* A very young chicken (baby chicken).

Pouter, *f.* A large-breasted pigeon.

Praliné, *f.* Flavoured with burnt almonds.

Pré-salé, *f.* Meat of prime mutton (Southdown mutton).

Pretty Toes. The feet of sucking pigs.

Printanier-(ère), *f.* Wherever this name is applied it always implies that a collection of early spring vegetables, left whole or cut small, is given, either as a garnish or in the form of macedoine. It is mostly used in connection with clear soups, removes and some ragoûts.

Profiteroles, *f.* A kind of light cake, baked in hot ashes, filled with cream.

Provençale (à la), *f.* A surname given to certain French dishes, which generally implies that garlic or onion and olive oil have been used in its preparation.

Prune, *f.* Plum, *e.* Name given to fresh and preserved fruit of the plum tree.

Ptarmigan, White Grouse, *e.* Perdrix blanche, *f.* In season September to April.

Pudding, *e.* Ponding, *f.* A sweet or a savoury, soft, and of convenient shape.

Puff-paste Patties, *e.* Bouchées, *f.*

Pulled Bread. Term applied to small pieces of bread; the crumb part of a loaf is pulled into pieces while hot, and baked in a moderate oven until they become crisp.

Pullet, *e.* Poulet, *f.* A young hen or female fowl.

Pumpernickel, *g.* Westphalian brown bread.

Punch. A species of hot drink.

Punch à la Romaine is a kind of soft white ice, made from lemon-juice, white of egg, sugar, and rum. It is served in goblets, usually after the remove; and it has the property of assisting considerably the functions of digestion. It forms a sort of interlude between two acts of that grand play—the dinner.

Purée, *f.* A smooth pulp; mashed vegetables; thick soups. The name is also given to meat or fish which is cooked, pounded in a mortar, and passed through a sieve.

Purslane is an American plant, used in salads, pot herbs, and pickles; first introduced into England in 1652.

Q.

Quab, *e.* A Russian river fish.

Quail, *e.* Caille, *f.* A bird of the grouse kind. Its flesh is very delicate and much esteemed by epicures.

Quark, *g.* Name of a German cheese, similar to curd cheese, known in France as "fromage mou."

Quart, *e.* The fourth of a gallon, two pints.

Quartier, *f.* Quarter, *e.* A fourth part.

Quartier d'Agneau. A quarter of lamb.

Quas, *f.* A Russian liquor, mostly used in the Russian army and navy. Is made of rye. Also called rye-beer.

Quasi de Veau, *f.* Name given to a piece of veal cut from the end of the loin.

Quenèfres, *f.* An Italian paste, somewhat similar to macaroni—used for soups, etc.

Quenelles, *f.* Forcemeat of different kinds, composed of fish, poultry or meat, eggs, etc., shaped in various forms—balls, ovals, etc. They are used as garnishing for soups or entrées, or are served separately as entrées.

Queue, *f.* Tail. " Queues de bœuf," " queues d'écrevisses." Ox-tail, crayfish tails, etc.

Quince, *e.* Coing, *f.* A sour astringent fruit, used for compôtes and marmalade.

Quoorma. Name of a very mild Indian curry preparation.

R.

Rabbit, *e.* Lapin, *f.* Its flesh, though inferior to that of the hare, has a more delicate flavour.

Radi, *f.* Radish, *e.* A salad plant with pungent root.

Rafraîchir, *f.* To refresh ; to cool.

Ragoût, *f.* A rich stew of meat, highly seasoned.

Raie, *f.* Skate, *e.* A flat sea fish. In season October to April.

Raifort, *f.* Horseradish, *e.* A root possessing a very pungent taste.

Raisin, *f.* Grape, *e.* The fruit of the vine, used as dessert, for jellies, ices, etc.

Raisins. Dried grapes, largely used for puddings, mince pies, also for dessert. The best raisins are imported from Turkey and Spain.

Ramequin, *f.* Ramakin, *e.* Cheese fritter ; a kind of cheese tartlet or ramakin.

Ramereau, *f.* Young wood pigeon.

Râper, *f.* To scrape or shred.

Raspberry, *e.* Framboise, *f.* A fruit allied to the bramble ; there are two kinds, the red and the white ; both are used for compotes, tarts and dessert.

Ratafie, or Ratafia. A culinary essence, being the essence of bitter almonds. A special kind of almond biscuits, in the shape of drops, are called ratafias. The name is also given to a liqueur flavoured with almonds.

Raton, *f.* A kind of cheesecake.

Ravigote, *f.* A very richly-flavoured green herb sauce; served cold. First heard of in 1720. A French writer, Ducereau, mentions it in one of his poems.

Ravioles, *f.* Small round paste dumplings, filled with forcemeat. Used as garniture for soups.

Réchauffé, *f.* Warmed-up meat recooked or redressed.

Red Cabbage, *e.* Chou rouge, *f.* A species of the common cabbage with dark red leaves, chiefly used for pickling. In Germany, France, and Switzerland it is prepared as a vegetable, when it is shredded finely and stewed in rich broth.

Red Grouse, or Moor Fowl, *e.* Perdrix rouge, *f.* A bird of exquisite flavour, sometimes called ptarmigan.

Red Herring. A fish principally eaten by the poorer classes.

Red Mullet, *e.* Rouget, *f.* A highly esteemed fish, called the woodcock of the sea. This fish should not be gutted; the trail is supposed to be eaten when cooked.

Réduire, *f.* To boil down; to reduce; to boil liquid gradually to a desired consistency.

Reindeer is a native of the Arctic regions, highly esteemed for its fine flavour. Reindeer tongues are a great delicacy, and now much appreciated in this country.

Reine Claude, *f.* Greengage, *e.* A fruit superior in richness and flavour to all other kinds of plums; name derived from Queen Claude, wife of Francis I.

Relevé, *f.* The remove, *e.* A course of a dinner, consisting of large joints of meat, four-footed game, and sometimes joints of fish.

Relever, *f.* To remove; to turn up.

Relish, *e.* Gout piquante. A pleasing taste; to give an excellent flavour.

Remouillage, *f.* Second stock, *e.*

Rémoulade, *f.* A cold sauce, flavoured with savoury herbs and mustard, used as salad-dressing, etc.

Renaissance, *f.* A word used for dishes of modern invention.

Rennet, *e.*, is the name given to the prepared inner membrane of a calf's, pig's, hare's, or fowl's stomach, which is used for curdling milk.

Restaurant, *f.* A high-class eating-house. Originally the name of a soup invented by a Frenchman named Palissy in 1557. The soup consisted of finely-minced fowl, and broth highly spiced with cinnamon, coriander, etc. In 1765 a tavern was opened in Paris, under the title "Restaurant," for the purpose of supplying this wonderful soup.

Réveillon, *f.* Name given to a gastronomic festivity which takes place in France at Christmas Eve. It consists of a sumptuous supper, which is provided by the most wealthy and the most generous inhabitants of a town or village. This meal is served at midnight, and the pièce de resistance is usually boudin noir —black pudding.

Rhubarb. A garden plant possessing a peculiar acid flavour, used for puddings, tarts, etc.

Rice, *e.* Riz, *f.* An esculent grain of warm climates, largely used throughout Europe for puddings and soups. Although highly nutritious, it is not a perfect food, being deficient in albuminoids and mineral matters.

Richelieu (Armand Jean). A celebrated gourmet. French general and cardinal during the reigns of Louis XIII and XIV; born 1585, died 1642.

Rillettes, *f.* A French savoury meat preparation, used for hors-d'œuvre and savouries.

Ris de Veau, *f.* (See SWEETBREAD, *e.*)

Risotto. An Italian dish of rice and cheese.

Rissolé (ée), *f.* Well browned, fried, or baked; covered with crumbs.

Rissoles, *f.* A mixture of minced fish or meat, enclosed in paste, half-moon shapes, and fried in fat or butter.

Rissolettes. Similar to rissoles; thin pancakes are used in place of paste.

Rizzered Haddie is the name of a Scotch dish, made from haddocks or codfish.

Roast (to), *e.*; Rôtir, *f.* Roasted, *c.*; Rôti(e), *f.* Roasting is one of the oldest and most favourite methods of cooking meat. It consists in hanging it in front of a bright fire, being suspended by means of a jack or spit. This process of cooking is very often performed in ovens, for which gas stoves are found most useful. Roasting means cooking by radiated heat.

Rob. From Arab, inspissated fruit juice of the consistency of honey.

Robert, *f.* Name of a brown spicy sauce, invented by a restaurant keeper of that name in Paris, 1789.

Robes de Chambre (en), *f.* (in dressing gown). Paper cases filled with light iced cream ; potatoes cooked and served in their jackets.

Rocket, *e.* A salad plant.

Roebuck, *e.* Chevreuil, *f.* A small species of deer.

Rognons, *f.* Kidney, *e.*

Romaine, *f.* Cos lettuce, *e.* À la Romaine, Roman style.

Romankeintjes. A Dutch pastry made of eggs, sugar, and almonds.

Roquefort, *f.* Roquefort, a highly-esteemed French cheese.

Rossini. Name of a famous musician. " Filets à la Rossini " was his own invention.

Rôti, *f.* The roast, *e.*, indicating the course of a meal which is served before the entremets. Roast meat, poultry, and game.

Roulade, *f.* Rolled meat smoked and cooked.

Roux, *f.* A preparation of butter and flour, used for thickening soups and sauces. There are three kinds of roux, white, fawn and brown.

Royaus. A delicately-flavoured small fish, similar to sardines, preserved in oil.

Royal. Name of an egg custard used for garnishing clear soups. Also the name applied to an icing (glace royale) made with whites of egg and icing sugar, and used for coating and decorative purposes.

Rump (of beef). The buttock ; the end of the backbone of beef.

S.

Sabayon, *f.* Pudding sauce, composed of cream or milk, sugar, white wine, and eggs.

Sack. The name of a wine used during the Middle Ages.

Sackposset. A drink made of sack (wine), milk, etc.

Safran, *f.* Saffron, *e.* A plant belonging to the species of crocus, native of Asia Minor, but largely cultivated in the South of Europe. It is used for colouring and flavouring in a number of culinary preparations.

Sago. The farina from the sago palm, a native of tropical countries. Sago is obtained from the trunk of this tree when slit open. It forms the chief food of the inhabitants of the Eastern Archipelago and other warm regions.

Saignant, *f.* Underdone, *e.*

Saindoux, *f.* Hog's lard. Used for frying and for modelling purposes. Socles, flowers, etc.

Salade, *f.* Salad, *e.* Raw herbs, edible plants, raw and cooked vegetables, etc., dressed with oil and vinegar.

Salamandre, *f.* This is an utensil which, after being made red-hot, is used for browning any dishes that want colour.

Salami. An Italian sausage.

Saler, *f.* To salt; to season with salt. " Saler de la viande "—to cure meat.

Saleratus is a kind of baking-powder consisting of potash, which is incorporated with an acid.

Salicoque. A small sea lobster of excellent taste.

Sally Luns, or Lunn. Name of a kind of tea-cake, slightly sweetened and raised with brewers' yeast. Sally Lunn was a pastrycook, who at the close of the eighteenth century used to make and sell a kind of tea-biscuits known as Sally Lunns. She used to sell these in the streets of Bath.

Salmagundi. Name of a very old English supper dish. It is a kind of meat-salad, mixed and decorated with hard-boiled eggs, anchovy, pickles and beetroot.

Salmi, or Salmis. A hash of game set to finish cooking when half roasted.

Salmon, *e.* Saumon, *f.* This delicious and most nutritive fish belongs to the finny tribe. It is found in the North of Europe and Asia; it never has been caught in the Mediterranean Sea. Seasonable March to August.

Salpicon. A mince of poultry or game, with ham,

tongue, and mushrooms; used for croquettes, bouchées, rissoles, etc.

Salsify, or Salsiflts. Sometimes called oyster plant. The flavour of the root resembles somewhat that of the oyster.

Salt, *e.* Du sel, *f.* The most needful and precious adjunct to our food.

Salzgurken is a German pickle, served with boiled or roast meats; made of cucumbers soused in salt water.

Samp. A food composed of coarsely ground maize, boiled and eaten with milk (American dish).

Sanbaglione is a delicious sweet chocolate cream; served in glasses either hot or cold.

Sandwich. A hors-d'œuvre. Two thin pieces of bread, buttered, with a thin slice of meat or edible paste between them. The name is supposed to be derived from the Earl of Sandwich.

Sangaree. The name of an Indian punch drink. It is made with sherry, water, lemon-juice, and sugar.

Sangler, *f.* To prepare the ice mixture ready for freezing. One part of salt to five parts of broken ice is the proper proportion used for freezing.

Sanglier, *f.* Wild boar, *e.*

Sapaceau. An egg punch.

Sapote, *f.* Sapota, *e.* A West Indian fruit.

Sarbotière, *f.* A pewter freezing pot or freezing pan.

Sarcelle, *f.* Teal, *e.* Water-fowl similar to wild duck. Seasonable October to February.

Sardine. A little fish, generally preserved in oil and packed in hermetically-closed tins or glass pots; served as a hors-d'œuvre, etc. Those caught on the French coast are considered to be the best.

Sarriette, *f.* Savoy cabbage, *e.*

Sassafras. The name of an agreeable beverage much drunk in North America.

Sasser, *f.* To stir rapidly with a spoon in a stewpan.

Sauce, *f.* Sauce, *e.* A liquid seasoning served and eaten with food, to improve its relish and to give flavour. The four great sauces in the culinary art are: Espagnole, Béchamel, Velouté, and Allemande.

Saucer, *f.* To sauce a dish; to cover with sauce.

Saucière, *f.* A sauceboat. A deep narrow-shaped dish in which sauce is served.

Saucisse, *f.* Fresh pork sausages.

Saucisson, *f.* Smoked sausages.

Sauerkraut, *g.* Choucroute, *f.* Sourkrout, *e.* A kind of pickled cabbage; cabbage preserved in brine. A national dish of Germany. Served hot with bacon or sausages.

Saugrenée, *f.* A French process of cooking, implying stewed with a little water, butter, salt, and herbs. Des pois à la saugrenée are stewed peas, cooked as above described.

Saumon, *f.* Salmon, *e.*

Saumoneau, *f.* Salmlet, *e.* A very small young salmon.

Saur, *f.* Smoke-dried, *e.* Saurer, *f.* To dry or cure in smoke.

Saurin, *f.* A freshly-cured herring.

Sauté-pan. Sautoire, *f.* A shallow thin-bottomed copper cooking pan.

Sauter (ée), *f.* To toss over the fire, in a sauté or frying-pan with little butter or fat, anything that requires a sharp fire and quick cooking.

Sauterne. A French white wine, much used in cookery.

Savarin (Brillat). Born 1755. Famous gastronomic writer; author of the excellent work entitled " Physiologie du Goût, ou Méditations de Gastronomie transcendante," published after his death. A light spongy yeast cake is named after him.

Saveloy. A kind of smoked pork sausage; it is highly seasoned, and has an addition of saltpetre to give the meat a red colour.

Scald. To scald milk is to bring it nearly to the boil.

Scallops, or **Escalop,** *e.* Pétoncles, *f.* A shellfish. This mollusc (mollusk) is similar in appearance to oysters, only much larger. Seasonable from September to March, and at its best during January and February. Only the muscular part or heart of a scallop is eaten. It is white, and when at its best the ova—or tongue, as it is commonly called—is full, and of bright orange colour. Scallops are prepared in numerous ways for the table : as stews in white sauce, scalloped, au gratin, sauté, as fritters, and sometimes in salads.

Schmorbraten, *g.* A German dish, consisting of rump of beef braised (à-la-mode fashion), garnished with mushrooms, gherkins, and braised vegetables.

Score (to). To make incisions crossways on the surface of fish, vegetables, or meat. This is done to facilitate the process of cooking, and thus improving the flavour.

Scorzonera. A kind of vegetable root; treated and served like parsnips or salsify.

Scotch Style. — l'Ecossaise, *f.*

Scots Kail. Name of a thick broth ; a kind of pot-au-feu, served as a standing dish among the middle classes of Scotland.

Seakale. As an article of diet, seakale is very little known on the Continent ; it grows wild in all parts of Europe. It was first grown in England in the middle of the eighteenth century by a gardener in Stoke Fleming, who cultivated the plants, which he found growing wild. They were so much appreciated that the gardener's master presented some of the roots to his friends at Bath, after which they became popular in all parts of England,

Seasoning, *e.* Assaisonnement, *f.* That which is used to render food palatable and more relishing. The word is also employed to include forcemeat and stuffing.

Seigle, *f.* Rye, *e.* Pain de seigle. Rye bread. This plant is indigenous to Southern Russia, but is now extensively grown in Germany, Scandinavia, and North America. Rye beer (see QUAS). Rye bread is very nutritious, and keeps fresh for a longer period than wheaten bread ; it is in use throughout the North of Europe.

Sel, *f.* Salt, *e.* (cloride of sodium). Used for seasoning food, for preserving and freezing purposes.

Seltz (Eau de Seltz), *f.* Seltzerwasser, *g.* A well known mineral water.

Semoule (Soujee), *f.* Semolina, *e.* The interior of hard and close-grained wheat.

Serviette, *f.* Table napkin, *e.* En serviette, served in a napkin, or dished up in a napkin.

Sévigné, *f.* A French soup named after the Marchioness Sévigné of Rabutin-Chantal, a French authoress, born 1626, died 1696.

Shank Jelly. A kind of savoury jelly, lightly seasoned, recommended to weak people.

Sherbet. A cooling drink consisting of water, lemon-juice and sugar. The word Sorbet is derived from Sherbet.

Sherry Cobbler. An American drink, made with soda-water, sherry, and sugar, a dash of liqueur, and a little ice.

Shin of Beef, *e.* Chinne de bœuf, *f.* The fore portion of a leg of beef. Used for stock, for making soups, etc.

Shot Pepper, *e.* This is mignonette pepper, which is made from white peppercorns. It is broken into grains or granulated about the size of mignonette seed.

Shred. Is to slice anything so finely with a sharp knife that the shreds curl.

Shrimp, *e.* Crevette, *f.* A small sea crustacean.

Shrub, *e.* Orange-juice, zest, and rum punch.

Sillsillat. A Swedish dish ; a kind of herring salad.

Simnel Cake. A Lenten or Easter cake, with raised crust, coloured with saffron, the interior being filled with the materials of a very rich plum pudding. They are made up very stiff, boiled in a cloth for several hours, then brushed over with egg, and baked.

Singe (Singeing), *e.* To pass a plucked bird over a flame so as to burn off the down which may have been left on. A spirit lamp is best for this purpose.

Singer. To dust with flour from the dredging-box.

Sippets. Small slices of bread cut into different forms, fried or toasted, served as garnishing with meat entrées, or for borders of savoury dishes.

Sirloin, *e.* Aloyau, *f.* The sirloin of beef is said to owe its name to King Charles II, who, dining off a loin of beef, and being well pleased with it, asked the name of the joint. On being told, he said, " For its merit, then, I will knight it, and henceforth it shall be called Sir Loin." In an old ballad this circumstance is thus mentioned :

> " Our Second Charles, of fame facete,
>   On loin of beef did dine ;
>   He held his sword, pleased, o'er the meat,—
>   ' Arise, thou famed Sir Loin.' "

Skewers for Joints, etc. Brochettes, *f.* Atelets, etc.

Skilly. The gruel or porridge given as nutriment to able-bodied paupers in workhouses.

Slapjack. Name of a special kind of pancakes.

Sling. A drink made of rum and water, sweetened.

Smelt, *e.* Eperlans, *f.* A most delicious little fish, its principal characteristic being the cucumber smell, which is most pronounced. The only legitimate way of cooking this fish is frying in deep fat. Usually served with lemon and thinly cut slices of brown bread and butter.

Snail (Edible). Escargot, *f.* Not much eaten in England, but in France it is considered a delicacy. The Romans esteemed it highly also.

Snipe, *e.* Bécasse, *f.* A small marsh bird.

Soja. An Indian flavouring sauce, very sharp.

Sole. A marine flatfish of most excellent flavour. Its flesh is white, delicate and nutritive.

Sorbet, *f.* An iced Turkish drink ; also the name of a water ice with fruit or liqueur flavour, usually served in goblets.

Sorrel, *e.* Oseille, *f.* A sour plant whose leaves are used for soups, and as a vegetable purée for garnish, etc.

Soubise, *f.* A smooth onion pulp served with various kinds of meat entrées. The name is supposed to come from Prince Charles Soubise (born 1715, died 1787), who was a celebrated epicure. He served as field marshal during the reign of Louis XIV of France. As a surname to dishes à la soubise is generally applied when onions enter largely into the composition of a dish ; the term implies that strong onion flavour, or a garnish of onion purée.

Soufflé, *f.* A very light baked or steamed pudding, an omelet. Also applied to light savoury creams.

Soufflé Glacé, *f.* A very light sweet cream mixture, iced and served in cases.

Sound. The air bladder of a fish.

Soup, *e.* Potage, *f.* Name applied to thick or clear soups.

Soy. The name of a dark brown sauce originally made in Japan ; there are many English relishes in which soy is employed as one of the ingredients.

Spaghetti. A kind of very small macaroni.

Spanish Style. À l'Espagnole, *f.*

Sparrowgrass. Old name for asparagus.

Spice, *e.* Epice, *f.* Condiment used for highly-seasoned food.

Spitchcock (to). To grill. (See SPREAD EAGLE.)

Sprat, *e.* Melettes, *f.* A small, cheap fish, allied to the herring.

Spread Eagle, *e.* Poulet à la Crapotine, *f.* A young fat chicken split down the back, flattened, breast-bone removed, seasoned, oiled or buttered, and grilled or baked.

Squab, *e.* A young pigeon ; name used particularly in North America. Squab chicken—a young chicken ; applicable to animals while young, fat, and clumsy. Squab pie is therefore primarily a (young) pigeon pie. Such a pie becomes Devonshire squab pie by the addition of apples. Squab-pigeons—innocents of French cooks.

Stake. Signifies small meal, breakfast, luncheon, lunch and tiffin. The word is supposed to be derived from " Steak," but is now very seldom used.

Steak means the slice of meat which is to be grilled, roasted or fried. Its Danish equivalent is Steeg, its German Stück (piece).

Stechi. A Russian oatmeal soup.

Stirabout. Name of an Irish dish similar to Scotch porridge.

Stock, *e.* Fond, *f.* The broth in which meat and bones have been boiled, of which soups and sauces are made.

Stove (to). To heat or bake in a stove or oven.

Succotash. An American dish made of green maize and baked beans. The dish is said to be borrowed from the Narraganset Indians, known to them as msickquatash.

Sucking Pig, *e.* Cochon de lait, *f.*

Sucre, *f.* Sugar, *e.* Sugar is obtained from various plants, but more especially from the sugar cane and the beetroot; but that obtained from other plants is absolutely identical, and differs in no respect from cane or beet sugars after being refined to the same degree of purity as those made from the latter plants. Science describes sugar to be a substance sweet to the taste, crystallisable and resolvable by fermentation into carbonic acid and alcohol. Dissolved in water and concentrated by heat we obtain syrups of various degrees according to requirements for culinary purposes. Pounded and sifted it is used for confectionery, pastry, cakes, puddings, etc. The use of sugar in its various forms covers a very extensive field, and its application it is said is still capable of further extension.

Suédoise (à la), *f.* Swedish style.

Supper, *e.* Souper, *f.* The last meal of the day.

Suprême, *f.* A rich, delicately flavoured cream sauce, made from chicken stock, etc.

Surlonge, *f.* Ancient name for sirloin.

Suzanne (Alfred). Name of a French chef, an authority on the culinary treatment of eggs. Author of " Egg Cookery: Over 150 Ways of Cooking and Serving Eggs," and " One Hundred Ways of Cooking Potatoes."

Sweetbread, *e.* Ris de Veau, *f.* Name given to the pancreas of a calf or lamb; considered the choicest part of the calf, and is regarded as a very great delicacy.

Sweet Dishes, *e.* Entremets (de douceur), *f.*

Syllabub. A kind of milk punch flavoured with liqueurs and spices. Usually served in glasses.

Syrup, *e.* Sirop, *f.* A saturated solution of sugar, generally flavoured with some fruit essence; used for various culinary purposes.

T.

Table d'Hôte. The table at which the principal meals at an hotel or restaurant are served to guests; a common table for guests; an ordinary.

Table Napkin, *e.* Serviette, *f.*

Tagliarini. A kind of macaroni paste cut in fine shreds.

Tailler la Soupe, *f.* A culinary expression. Thin slices or crusts of bread placed in a soup tureen are called tailler. "Tremper la soupe" is the French term applied when the broth is poured over the slices.

Taillevent. Name of a clever artist in cookery who superintended the kitchens of Charles VII of France from 1430 to 1461. Inventor of a sweet soup, called "potage doré," the recipe of which is anything but recommendable for the present time.

Talleyrand. Several high-class dishes are styled thus. The name comes from an old French ducal family.

Talmouses, *f.* A kind of French pastry, sweet or savoury, made in the shape of parsons' caps.

Tamarind. The name of a tropical tree and its fruit, which is used for condiments, sauces, etc.

Tamis, *f.* Tammy, *e.* Woollen canvas cloth which is used for straining soups and sauces.

Tansy, *e.* A herb with strong aromatic flavour, sometimes used for flavourings in puddings.

Tapioca. The substance obtained from the roots of the cassava (manioc plant), a native of the tropical parts of Asia, America and Africa. Brazil exports the most to this country. Tapioca is considered to be one of the most easy digestive farinaceous foods, and is therefore recommended for invalids and children.

Tarragon, *e.* Estragon, *f.* Aromatic plant used for flavouring; also for flavouring vinegar.

Tart. From the Latin *torta,* a baked ring of twisted dough, which was laid round and eaten with cooked fruit. The name now includes a great number of cakes of a complicated kind.

Tartare, *f.* A cold sauce, made of yolks of eggs, oil, mustard, capers, gherkins, etc., served with fried fish or cold meats; also a salad dressing.

Tartaric Acid. This is an acid which exists in a great many kinds of fruit, though it is chiefly obtained and extracted from the grape root. It is used for similar purposes as citric acid, and has the same effect on sugar.

Teal, *e.* Sarcelle or Sercelle, *f.* Water-fowl.

Tench, Tanche, *f.* A fresh-water fish, allied to the carp. Seasonable December to February.

Tendrons, *f.* Name applied to gristles of veal, etc.

Terrapin. Small American turtle, very little known and used in this country.

Terrine, *f.* China pan or pot, used for pâtés and for potted meats.

Tête de Veau, *f.* Calf's head, *e.*

Therid. An Arab word for a soup. Principal ingredients used are : broth, olive oil, eggs, vinegar and breadcrumbs.

Thon, *f.* Tunny, *e.* A sea-fish preserved in oil or marinade, mostly used as hors-d'œuvre.

Thyme. An aromatic plant used as seasoning.

Tiffin. The name given in India to the repast taken between ten and eleven o'clock in the morning.

Timbale, *f.* Literally " kettle-drum " ; a kind of crusted hash baked in a mould.

Toast. Dried, grilled or scorched slices of bread.

Tobasco. Name of a savoury Indian sauce.

Toddy. An American punch.

Tokai, *f.* Tokay, *e.* A Hungarian wine.

Tom and Jerry. An American drink ; an egg punch.

Tomatoes, *e.* Tomates, *f.* Also called love-apples (pommes d'amour), from the Italian pomi di mori (apples of the moors).

Tomber à Glace, *f.* To reduce a liquid until it has the appearance of a thick syrup.

Tonalchile. Guinea pepper.

Topinambours, *f.* Jerusalem artichokes, *e.*

Tortue, *f.* Turtle, *e.* Also called Sea Tortoise.

Toulouse (à la), *f.* A rich white stew of white meats, mushrooms, truffles, etc., used for filling crusts or for garnishing.

Tournedos, *f.* Small thin fillets of beef served as entrées. First served in Paris in 1855.

Tourner, *f.* To stir a sauce ; also to pare and cut roots.

Tourte, *f.* An open tart baked in a round shallow tin.

Tourtelettes, *f.* Small tartlets, *e.*

Tranche, *f.* Slice, *e.* Mostly applied to salmon, cod, etc.

Trancher, *f.* To cut ; to carve.

Trautmannsdorff. Name of an Austrian Count, born 1749, died 1827. Several sweets are styled after his name.

Trifles. A dish of sweetmeats and cake. A second course dish of cakes, biscuits, jams, etc.

Trim, *e.* To pare ; to cut off portions of meat or vegetables in order to improve their appearance.

Tripe. The prepared and boiled stomach and alimentary canal of oxen and other animals.

Trousser, *f.* To truss a bird.

Trout, *e.* Truite, *f.* Fresh-water fish, seasonable May to August.

Truffer, *f.* To garnish a sauce with truffles, or to season the interior of poultry or game with truffle stuffing, such as capons, turkeys, and pheasants.

Truffles, *e.* Truffes, *f.* A fungus of the same order as the mushroom. They grow in clusters of an irregular globular form under roots of young trees (oak, nut, and a few other trees). There are three kinds—the black, the grey, and the red. The latter is musk-scented, and very rare. The former two are mostly used for garnish and other culinary purposes. The South and West of France produce the best kinds. Trained pigs and dogs are employed to find truffles. Périgueux and Carpentras are the most famous districts in France.

Truite Saumonée, *f.* Salmon trout, *e.*

Turban, *f.* Ornamental entrées of chicken and forcemeat, dressed in the form of a turban, which verbally means a hair-dress worn in the East.

Turbot, a flat fish ; its flesh possesses a delicate flavour and is wholesome. In season March to August.

Turkey, *e.* Dinde, *f.* A large species of domestic fowl.

Turn, *e.* To trim or pare vegetables into neat round or oval shapes.

Turn-broche, or **Turnspit.** Formerly joints while being roasted were turned by young persons or trained dogs ; now they are turned by clockwork previously wound up.

Turnips, *e.* Navets, *f.* A white bulbous root.

Turtle. The turtle was first brought to England in the middle of the seventeenth century. Its first appearance as an edible dish is repulsive. We learn from Sir Hans Sloane that at the beginning of the last century turtle was only eaten in Jamaica by the poor.

Tutti-frutti. An Italian expression for various kinds of fruits, or a mixture of cooked vegetables.

Twelfth Cake. A large cake, into which a bean, ring or other article was introduced, made for Twelfth Night festivals. The cake being cut up, whosoever got the piece containing the ring or bean was accepted as king for the occasion.

Tyrolienne (à la), *f.* Tyrolean style.

U.

Ude (Louise Eustache). A famous chef, at one time cook to Louis XVI and the Earl of Sefton. Author of the "French Cook."

Usquebagh. The name of an Irish beverage, consisting of a compound spirit made with spices and sugar.

V.

Vandreuil, *f.* An excellent fish, found principally at the sea-side of the French dept. Provence.

Vanille, *f.* Vanilla, *e.* The fruit of a fragrant plant; the most delicate flavouring for all kinds of sweet dishes.

Vanille (à la), *f.* Vanilla-flavoured.

Vanneau, *f.* Plover; lapwing; pewit.

Vanner, *f.* To stir a sauce quickly, so as to work it up lightly, in order to make it smooth.

Vatel. Name of a clever and ingenious chef, who acted in that capacity to Louis XIV of France. He took his life because the fish for a special banquet did not arrive in time. Dishes "à la Vatel" are much appreciated.

Veau, *f.* Veal, *e.* The flesh of the calf.

Vegetables, *e.* Légumes, *f.*

Velouté, *f.* A rich white sauce. Foundation sauce.

often used to improve the flavour of soups or made dishes.

Venaison, *f.* Venison, *e.* The flesh of the deer.

Vénitienne (à la), *f.* Venetian style, *e.*

Vermicelle, *f.* Vermicelli, *it.* Very fine rolls of paste, made from the dough of wheat flour, and forced through cylinders or pipes till it takes a slender worm-like form, when it is dried ; used in soups, puddings, and for crumbing.

Vert-pré, *f.* Name of a green herb sauce.

Vésicaire, *f.* Winter cherry, *e.*

Viande, *f.* Meat, viands, *e.* Meat, dressed victuals.

Viennoise (à la). Vienna or Viennese style.

Villeroux. The name of a chef, a friend of the great Carême, who was famous as Count Mirabeau's chef. It is said that Villeroux went to live among a wild tribe in India, where he practised his art with such success that within a very short time he was proclaimed king. When he died, he left his people as a legacy the recipe for making " Omelette au Jambon." If the statement be true, it is the only instance in history of a cook being made a king. Villeroux's biographer describes him as a worthy prince, who was celebrated, not only as a cook, but also for his wit and love of adventure. This accounts, probably, for his falling into the midst of a wild Indian tribe.

Vin blanc (au), *f.* Done in white wine.

Vinaigre, *f.* Vinegar, *e.* *Vinaigrer,* to season with vinegar.

Vinaigrette, *f.* A sauce of vinegar, oil, pepper, and herbs.

Volaille, *f.* Poultry, *e.*

Vol-au-vent, *f.* A light round puff paste crust, filled with delicately flavoured ragoûts of chicken, sweetbread, etc. (*à la financière*).

Volière. Birdcage style of dressing poultry or game.

Vopallière. A dish of small chicken fillets, larded and braised, served with truffle sauce.

Vraie tortue, *f.* Real turtle, *e.*

W.

Wafers, *e.* Waffeln, *g.* Gauffres, *f.* A kind of light and thin paste crust, either baked, fried or grilled. The meaning of the word, which is of Teutonic origin, is honey-comb.

Walnut. Originally imported from Persia, is generally served with fruits as dessert.

Wastle Cake, Scotch. Wastle bread was baked on a girdle, which is analogous to the English girdle or griddle cake.

Water, *e.* Eau, *f.* A transparent fluid composed of oxygen and hydrogen. Water cannot be classified as food, for it produces neither heat nor force, though without it all vital action would come to a standstill.

Watercress. An aquatic plant, used for salads, etc.

Weever. A fish of the perch family.

Welsh Rarebit. Commonly called Welsh rabbit. A slice of toasted bread covered with melted cheese and butter, seasoned with pepper and mustard.

Whelk, *e.* A shellfish, called the poor man's delicacy, known to be most indigestible as a food.

Whey, *e.* Petits lait, *f.* The coagulated portion of milk, used as a cooling beverage.

Whitebait, *e.* Blanchailles, *f.* The smallest known species of the herring genus. When fried they form one of the most appreciated dishes of the " haute cuisine." Owing to their great delicacy they ought to be cooked as fresh as possible. Slices of lemon and thinly cut brown bread and butter are always handed round with this fish. Seasonable February to May.

Whitepot, *e.* An ancient preparation of cream, eggs, pulp of apples, etc., etc., baked in a dish or in a crust. This is a kind of custard fruit purée pie, verging towards a charlotte.

White Stew, *e.* Blanquette, *f.*

Whiting, *e.* Merlans, *f.* Fish seasonable March to August.

Widgeon, *e.* Sarcelle, *f.* Seasonable October to February.

Woodcock, *e.* Coq du bruyère, *f.* Seasonable October to December.

X.

Xanthurus. An East-Indian fish, resembling the carp; known in the Dutch colonies as "geelstard."

Xavier. Name of a clear soup. Supposed to have been introduced by King Louis XVIII in honour of Count Xavier of Saxony, who died in 1806.

Xeres. Spanish strong wine of deep amber colour and aromatic flavour; so called from Xeres, a place near Cadiz.

Y.

Yeast, *e.* Levain; levure, *f.* Also called barm. It is added in small quantities to flour for making dough intended to ferment, in order to quicken the process.

Yorkshire Rarebit. A Welsh rarebit (toasted bread and cheese), with a slice of broiled bacon and a poached egg on top.

Young Wild Boar, *e.* Marcassin, *f.*

Z.

Zabyajone, *it.* A frothing mixture of wine, yolks of eggs, and sugar, thickened over the fire, and served hot in glasses.

Zambaglione. A kind of chocolate creams; served in glasses, either hot or cold.

Zéphire, *f.* Name of small oval-shaped forcemeat dumplings, a kind of quenelles, which are poached and served with a rich sauce.

Zuppa al Brodo. A fish broth with toasted bread and cheese.

Zythogala. Græcified name applied by Sydenham, the English physician, and later by the French doctor Secquet, to the then popular posset (etc., etc.).

Zythum, or **Zythos.** A liquid made from malt and wheat; a kind of malt beverage.